W2.

Published by
Um Peter Publishing

ISBN 978-1-50256-491-7

Also available as a Kindle ebook
ISBN 978-1-84396-321-9

Pre-press production
www.ebookversions.com

Acknowledgements

Rebecca Hall – author of *Fruits of Paradise* (Simon & Schuster, 1993), *Animals Are Equal* (Rider) and others – for her kindness and invaluable suggestions.

The many friends who read and commented on the early drafts.

Readers' comments

"I have never read a book that is so personal yet so eye-opening in terms of the country and its people." – *Victoria Morris*

"This is a unique way of seeing, feeling and reacting. Through the wisdom of choosing love, humanity, calm, perseverance in challenging times of hardship. It leads the way through the barren lands of misunderstanding and the unfamiliar. It is more than a book. It is a source of understanding." – *Sofie Andersson*

"I was so fascinated that I couldn't put it down… I learned so much, I hope that other people will get the opportunity to do the same." – *Pat Wheelhouse*

"These anecdotes create a picture of a social organisation that is tribal in practice while having to relate to aspects of western influence." – *Barry Henderson*

The writing is so beautifully descriptive that I can see it all happening and even smell the food!" – *Liz Williams*

My Petra
family

My friend and guide
Bassam Ali

His mother
H'Layla

His sisters
Wotha   R'Kheeya

His brothers
Ahmed   Majid   Nasser   Khalil   Sa'ood
(half]

His wife
Fatma

Her mother
Hamda

Her sisters
Zaynab   Hadeeja
So'mah   Tamam   H'Layla   Aisha

Her brothers
Mohammed   Adel   Ali   Faisal

Bassam Ali's and Fatma's children
Chowfa   Jasmine   Ahmed   Ayeesha   Abdullah

(As a courtesy, some names have been changed.)

LIVING
with
ARABS

Nine years with
the Petra Bedouin

JOAN WARD

UM PETER PUBLISHING

Contents

Chapter 1
An Alien World

It was a quiet afternoon in October 2008. I had been in the country for four years and was well settled in the Bedouin village of Um Sayhoun at Petra. The peace that afternoon was broken by the rising sound of jeering boys. That was not unusual. Sometimes their prey was a puppy, sometimes a sick donkey. That particular afternoon, the object of their attention was a 13-year-old boy called Faisal.

I knew this boy. He was my neighbour's nephew. He was tall for his age, but much of his height was lost to deformity. He had the appearance of one who suffers from cerebral palsy. He walked with difficulty, lop-lopsidedly, because one of his feet had a growth of bone on the sole. He stooped. His forearms drooped, his head dipped onto his chest and his tongue constantly hung out. He couldn't speak. The only things that emerged from his mouth were grunts and a constant stream of saliva.

That afternoon he had strayed from his home. He was usually locked in an inner room if his mother or sister needed to be out. As I looked from my window into the wadi below my house, I could see that he was being driven further from his home by a pack of about 20 boys aged between 4 and 12 years. As I watched, two boys threw stones at him, herding him as they would one of their goats. A car drew up on the dusty track alongside them. The driver got out, saw what was happening and shouted at the boys. They started to scatter and I hoped against hope that Faisal's trial had ended. It hadn't. The man went into his house without looking back to see if his instructions were being followed. They weren't. The moment his back was turned, the boys regrouped.

I had to do something. In the privacy of my home, I was wearing a sleeveless T-shirt. If I were to have any chance of imposing my will on the pack, I needed to cover my arms. By the time I got outside, Faisal was climbing up my side of the wadi and approaching my garden wall. Just like a grotesque version of *What's the Time Mr Wolf,* the boys pursued him, cruelly baiting. They were occasionally rewarded by his turning and growling at them. Their squeals of delight were attracting the women and girls from their homes to spectate. I locked my door and moved towards them, shouting,

"Shoo yamaloo? What are you doing?" I was totally ignored. As I approached, I could see that the tops of Faisal's buttocks were exposed by the slippage of his ill-fitting, second-hand track-suit bottoms. The other boys were having a field day.

By the time that I caught up with them, Faisal was sitting on the kerb of the main road through the village surrounded by jeering boys, with at least eight women with younger children and girls looking on, smiling. I went and sat on the curb beside him. That, at least, stopped the stones. My hope was that he would let me hold his hand and escort him home, some 50 metres away. At that moment, one of the boys shouted abuse that caused Faisal to rise and lunge at them. They ran away as he pursued them into the warren of narrow back streets. I followed and found him sitting on the ground against a wall.

A twenty year old woman called Noor approached. She,

Um Sayhoun

too, was not afraid to stand alone in the face of these boys and our condoning neighbours. She agreed to stay with Faisal while I went to get my car. Within two minutes, I was back. The group of children had grown to around thirty. I got out of my car and walked towards Faisal. I shouted in Arabic,

"This is not television. Go to your homes." The women looked on, smiling. No. This was better than television.

I turned to Faisal and said, "Hello Faisal. Would you like to get into my car?" By the grace of God, he rose docilely and climbed into the front passenger seat. I went around to my side, got in and started the engine. The poor boy stank so badly that I could scarcely breathe. I had not gone five metres, when it became clear that the pack was planning to follow us up the road. This would have been easy because there were five fierce speed bumps on that 50

3

metre stretch. So, speed wasn't an option. I stopped the car, got out, went round to the back and faced them. I shouted as loud as I could so that all their mothers could hear.

"*Hiwonaat assan minkum. Rooah al beytkum*! Animals are better than you. Go to your homes!" I wanted to say, "You are worse than animals," but I didn't know the Arabic word for 'worse'. Silence and stillness fell. I turned and drove away.

Faisal enjoyed the journey home. When we arrived, he waited for me to get out, go around to his side and open the door for him. Out he climbed and returned to the safety of his home. His mother was sitting on the floor preparing food for the evening meal. His 17 year old sister gave him three heavy thumps on his back with her clenched fists before I had time to tell her about his suffering. Faisal's father and mother were first cousins. His father had died four weeks previously, aged 47 years. The family was poor. There were six other children, two of whom had severe learning difficulties. Everyone in the village knew their trouble. Every boy in that pack knew who Faisal was and that his family was in mourning.

What kind of place was this? What sort of people were these? What kind of men do these boys become? Why did the women do nothing that day? What was important in their lives? What did they value? What did they despise?

In the years that followed this incident, it became possible to answer these questions, at least partially. Faisal never forgot me and my car. On several occasions I saw him, in danger, walking down the centre of the road outside the village. I always stopped. He always got in and let me take him home. From time to time he would just sit in the road next to my parked car, waiting for me. He took exception to the silver UPVC car cover that I used at the height of summer. More than once, he tried to remove the offending material, only to get it caught under the registration plate. A huge hole appeared in the front forming a useless loop of elasticated hem drooping in the dust.

The courageous Noor is now a beautiful woman of 25 years. Unusually, she still lives at home. Some years ago, a young man came and asked her father for her. The father knew him to be a drinker and he was refused. She keeps largely out of sight these days, behind the high walls of her father's house, waiting, like many other women, for someone else to come and ask for her.

Chapter 2
The Start Of It All

In January 2004, I visited Jordan for the first time as a tourist. One day, we were visiting an archaeological dig at a Neolithic village just north of Petra. It wasn't a spectacular place. We were on the edge of a wide, barren wadi, with our view of the Petra mountains obscured by a rock face. The guide, Ahmad, suddenly looked at me with such a steady gaze and said,

"Do you like it here?" I couldn't answer immediately. I was thinking of being honest and replying that this particular spot wasn't especially beautiful. In the time that it took for that thought to arise and be dismissed, my heart lurched with the realization that this place was my soul's home. I wanted to stay here forever. I can only describe the feeling as visceral.

"Yes," I said, "I do." Such simple words but they turned my life upside down.

I was a teacher at a prestigious boys' school in West Sussex, with a year to go to my retirement. I was happy in my job, my salary was good and I felt that I was on the home straight. Instead, on my return from holiday, I emailed a company which recruits UK-trained teachers for schools overseas, asking if they had any vacancies in

Amman. The managing director telephoned me the very next day and said,

"You are too old to work in Jordan but I could offer you two years in the British Virgin Islands." I didn't want to go to the BVI and I waited for the world to turn. After that, I returned to Jordan in the February half term, the Easter holiday and the May half term. Two days before I was due to fly home in May, I received a telephone call from the Principal of the International Community School in Amman. Could I attend an interview in Amman on the following day? I was appointed Head of English on a two-year contract. The world had turned, as I somehow knew that it would.

Those early holidays and the weekends of the two years that I taught in Amman, were spent on donkey back in the Petra mountains, accompanied by a wonderful guide, whose family were to become my closest friends and neighbours. Bassam Ali had two white donkeys and two mules. His home was in Um Sayhoun, the village created by the Jordanian Government when they wanted to develop Petra as a tourist site. His people had been living in the tombs and caves of Petra for as long as anyone could remember. In the 1970s, His Majesty King Hussein himself came down to Petra, to explain to the Bedouin why they must move from their homes. The new village would have three distinct advantages; running water, electricity and schools for the girls and boys. Most of the boys had been going to school but not the girls. In 2004, few women over 25 years could read or write. They could simply count.

The word "village" implies something attractive and homely. Um Sayhoun is neither. It is a collection of breeze-block units, little better than caves with light sockets, electricity points and taps. Those who want hot water buy geysers. Not everyone bothers. Many families, including

Bassam Ali's, herd their goats in the mountains and grow wheat in the few pockets of stony soil. Often the men, sometimes with their families, will eat their evening meals in the mountains, around a fire, away from the village, with many preferring to sleep there too when they can. Even in the village, many people sleep outdoors for most of the year, under colourful Chinese fleece blankets and frames of mosquito nets.

Only those in the city centre of ancient Petra were required to move. Off the beaten tourist track, many families still live in tombs and caves, getting their water from Government-provided stand pipes. There are children who travel to school in the village each day from these outlying areas. The lucky ones have donkeys. On foot, their journeys could take an hour or more.

On one of those early weekends, Bassam asked me if I would like to go to a Bedouin wedding - at least the first

Saloom's Beda home

9

part of the celebration, when the groom's family and friends come together two days before the bride comes from the village. I jumped at the chance and was taken to a Bedouin encampment well off the tarmac road. Bassam deposited me at the women's tent and said, "Sit by the fire with those old women. They are nice."

Indeed they were. Their names were Saloom and Hamda and they were two of the great matriarchs of the Petra Bedouin. Neither spoke a word of English. Saloom had given birth to fourteen children. Her first two, both girls, died in infancy. Years later, as she told me about the way each of their heads had been stitched together following the post mortem, and how she had wrapped their bodies for the last time, her eyes welled with tears. Her husband of fifty years, Juma, had never taken another wife. I was to become a frequent visitor at their hearth. [Juma sadly died two years ago. He had suffered a heart attack after helping his sons move both his and his widowed neighbour's goats-hair homes to their winter sites. He was a magnificent man.]

Hamda had been a widow for many years. She had given birth to a similar number of children. I was never quite sure exactly how many. Seven years later, I visited her in hospital two weeks before she died. Her head was uncovered and her wispy hair was orange from applications of henna to hide her grey hairs. What a character. Hamda, too, had been her husband's only wife. Both women were very proud of this.

They greeted me warmly and settled me on a raffia mat by the fire. After half an hour, they could see that it was difficult for me to sit on the floor with my back unsupported. All the other women and girls were sitting perfectly comfortably, cross-legged. Even in my youth my body had been incapable of maintaining that position for

Saloom's husband, Juma.

long. School assemblies in my junior years had been complete trials.

Saloom and Hamda went away and returned with a thin mattress and a hard cushion. They insisted, by signs and unintelligible words, that I should not only sit on the mattress but should swing my feet around onto it and lie down with my elbow on the cushion. The agony temporarily abated. Despite the discomfort and the enforced silence, I realised very quickly that I needed to show by my body language and my facial expression that I honoured what I saw and that I was comfortable in their company.

After a while, I noticed a toddler making her way towards me across the dirt floor. She was ten or eleven months old and was wearing a very grubby, overlarge bridesmaid's dress. I was sitting with my legs stretched out, supported by my hands behind me. She climbed onto my shins, turned and climbed up my body until her face, with mucus streaming from her nose, was four inches from mine. Several of the women watched her progress and then made comments to each other. I couldn't understand, of course, but I instinctively knew that it was a watershed moment. Animals and small children can "smell" whom they can trust and here was this little one demonstrating just that. The kindly eyes of the old women became even warmer. We had a good game, the little girl and I, as I moved her feet to the rhythm of the drums.

I sat on that thin mattress for two hours. It was becoming almost unbearable when the men finally produced the food. All the men would have eaten and only after they had all finished would the women be served. The meal was served on large, shallow, circular trays of three feet diameter. There was room for eight to ten women and children around each one. The women quickly arranged themselves in groups and a plastic jug of water and a small packet of Tide washing powder were brought for us to wash our hands. The food was *mansaf*, a traditional Jordanian dish served at both special occasions and family meals. One or more goats would have been slaughtered on makeshift tripods made of sticks. The men will have skinned the goats and then butchered them. The pieces of meat, including the goats' heads, are put in a huge pot of boiling salted water. After a couple of hours, goats' milk yoghurt is added. The serving tray is lined with *shrak*, a wonderful form of unleavened bread which the women throw on circular, domed, metal dishes over an open fire. Then the boiled rice is added, followed by the meat pieces in the yoghurt sauce. For special occasions like this, chopped parsley and fried peanuts are scattered on the top. *Salat Arabi,* which is a mixture of diced cucumber and tomatoes, sprinkled with salt and lemon juice, is served as a side dish.

I managed to take my place at a tray, taking up twice the room of a Bedouin woman because I couldn't sit cross-legged, *and* lean forward to eat. I found it extremely difficult to tear off pieces of bread with one hand. I got better at it later on, pinning one side down with my little finger while the others fingers pulled a piece away. However, I was very hungry and I somehow managed. I used the bread to pick up a piece of meat. It was dark by then and we were eating by firelight. Using my fingertips, I tried to ensure that I had a fibrous piece of meat and not a piece of gristle or, worse still, one of the eyes or offal. When I say 'offal' I do not mean liver or kidney. I would have been grateful to have found a piece of either of those! The meat of the goat is rather rich so, after 3-4 pieces I settled for dipping the bread pieces in the sauce.

When we had finished eating and the water and Tide had reappeared, the men rounded up some of the younger women to do the washing up. At that point, Bassam Ali arrived to take me back to my hotel. These people are lovely. My admiration for the women is almost beyond words. One particular woman in her mid to late thirties had been sitting to my right all evening. She was very beautiful with lovely eyes and a fine bone structure. However, she had absolutely no teeth. During the evening, she had been breast-feeding her sixteenth child.

Chapter 3

A Mountain Lunch

In Jordan, as in all Moslem countries, the weekend begins on Thursday afternoon. Each Thursday after school, I would climb into my car with a weekend case already packed and head south. Petra is three hours' drive from Amman. Most of that journey is on the Desert Highway, the most easterly of the three north-south routes in Jordan. The Desert Highway is largely dual carriageway but I would not want to give the impression that it is an easy drive. The speed limit for cars is 110 kph. Communities of strip development punctuate this road. The speed limit stays the same.

Traffic is controlled by speed bumps. In those early days, these were heavily disguised, being as black as the surrounding road, and unannounced by any warning signs. My car was a 1999 Daiwoo Lanos. It was an incredibly faithful machine whose back I nearly broke more than once as I flew over unseen bumps. I eventually memorized the positions of these *m'tabat*. The winter months presented even more of a challenge. There were no cats' eyes and very few white lines to define the centre and edges of the road. The kind receptionists at the Crowne Plaza in Wadi Musa, who had got to know me as a frequent visitor, were in the habit of telephoning me.

"Are you all right?" they would say.

"Yes. I've just turned off the Desert Highway." They would know then that I was forty minutes away.

One Friday, the Sabbath, my Bedouin guide, Bassam Ali, planned to take me to a mountain area called Garoon. It lies on the edge of the Petra mountains overlooking Wadi Araba some 1,500 metres below. This is a northern extension of the great east African rift valley and is home to what is left of the River Jordan.

We left Bassam's house in the Bedouin village at 8.30am. He said,

"I will take some chicken and we will make lunch up there..." I always rode a wonderful white donkey called Azuz and Bassam took one of his mules. Ahead of us was two hours' riding in temperatures ranging, as the sun arose, from 24-32 degrees. I was born and bred in Birmingham. I remembered having ridden donkeys as a child at Rhyl and Weston-Super-Mare on Sunday-School outings and maybe once or twice on a family holiday in North Devon. That was the full extent of my riding experience. However, I discovered that I had been blessed with a built-in microchip, giving me the confidence and skills to ride. Azuz was a tall donkey and I felt very high up there on his back. I took comfort and gained confidence from the realisation that his centre of gravity was much lower than mine, and that he had four points of contact with the ground. The single most important thing, therefore, was to stay in contact with him, ideally on his back.

Our journey took us over apparently barren terrain, criss-crossed by wadis, dried water courses, of varying depths. Sometimes we could ride directly down and up across the wadi. At others which were very steep with shale-like slippery sides, we needed to make a detour around the head of the wadi. No steering was required from me. Azuz was his own satnav, encouraged by frequent clicks of the tongue from Bassam. The land is semi-desert with brush and isolated juniper and pistachio trees. The most common wild animals are lizards, which skittered away as we approached. Some of them have amazing turquoise-blue heads.

We passed three flocks of goats. Two were tended by women, the other by a man whom Bassam greeted. The sound of the flute could often be heard. The flutes are home-made, sometimes from sections of bamboo, sometimes from something as simple as a section of hose. I asked if the music was a way of controlling the goats. The sound seemed so haunting, redolent of snake-charming. The answer was No.

"They have no one to talk to, so they play" Bassam said.

"Ah," I replied. "Is that why you start singing when we haven't spoken for half an hour?" Much laughter.

Sometimes I had to dismount at the top of the wadis, where one watershed gave way to another – rather like mountain passes. This particular day, we had passed just

The writer on Azuz

such a place when we came upon a group of men, fairly high on a rocky ledge. I naively thought that they were painting some words of protest on the rock face because red paint seemed to be running down the rocks. On closer inspection, I realised that they had set up a make-shift tripod and had, indeed, just slaughtered a goat and were busy skinning it. We shouted greetings and they asked us to stay and have lunch. Bassam explained that we didn't have time, and we went on our way. At that time I was not vegetarian but, even so, my very being recoiled from the ease with which the life of the animal had been snuffed out. I later realised that the diet of the Bedouin was relatively limited and that their animals provided much-needed protein and iron.

We reached Garoon at about 10.30. Despite the heat-haze, the view was breathtaking. Below us were tent-like domes of weathered sandstone, occasionally interrupted by blacker, more angular basalt outcrops. 1,500 metres below us, the flat wadi floor comes sharply up to the edge of the mountains. There are no foothills here. The River Jordan long ago ceased flowing at this latitude but the line of it could still be seen from the sparse vegetation along what had been its banks. This is the Jordan-Israeli border and the mountains which form the western edge of the Wadi Araba were clearly visible. My mobile phone pinged, welcoming me to Israel.

After we had rested and enjoyed the view, we started to prepare lunch. Bassam announced that the goatherd whom we had passed was going to join us for lunch. Fairly unusually, he was a man on his own. His parents lived in a Bedouin tent, but his wife preferred to live in the village. His mother used to look after the goats but his father had become incapacitated and so she needed to remain in the tent with him.

The first job in preparing the lunch was collecting wood. Usually, when we stopped to make bedouin tea, the dried twigs which lie loose on the ground are sufficient but today, Bassam was taking larger branches from a nearby juniper. They were low and drooping, just ready to be used. He picked up a large boulder and smashed it down on the chosen branch. The Bedouin are extremely resourceful and are masters of improvisation. No hammer? Use a disused engine part. No tea-glass? Cut the top or bottom off a plastic water bottle. No tripod for the pot? Use stones.

Bassam soon had quite a blaze going. Meanwhile I was peeling and slicing potatoes, tomatoes, onions, garlic and green pepper. My chopping board was the black plastic bag that had carried the vegetables and my blade was a Swiss army knife that I had brought from England as a highly-prized gift for Bassam. All these things Fatma, Bassam's wife, had packed for us, along with twists of salt, black pepper and spices. Bassam produced a largely still-frozen chicken from one of the saddle bags. He pulled the legs out from the body, handed me one and asked me to hold it "like a goat." With the memory of the slaughter still fresh in my mind, I realised that he needed me to create some tension so that he could cut the chicken into portions. He got eight good pieces out of it, which he duly skinned. Meanwhile, I was concentrating on trying to sanitise my hands, having unexpectedly handled the raw chicken.

A roll of aluminium foil appeared and was spread on the ground. First he arranged some sliced potatoes. Then he layered the chicken and the rest of the ingredients. The salt, pepper and spices were sprinkled on the top and then, between us, we made a very tidy gift-wrapped parcel. Using a long branch, he spread the white-hot embers, put the parcel in the middle of the fire and then, using a thin, flat rock, carefully lifted the embers and covered the foil. He then scraped what was left of the fire around the sides of the silver parcel.

"That will take an hour," he said.

A half an hour later we could see, in the distance, our lunch guest on his way to join us. It took him 25 minutes to reach us. He was dressed in western clothes, as was Bassam, and had his mobile on his belt. This was unusual. Most of the people in the mountains, both men and women, wear traditional Bedouin dress. When the lunch was ready, Bassam found a large flat stone, dug it under the parcel of food and lifted it away from the fire. He had some soft, fine twigs which he used to sweep the ash from the top. He then put his face very close to the foil and blew away the remaining ash particles before carefully starting to expose the food.

A delicious smell hit our noses as the steam escaped. It was a platter fit for a king. The vegetables which had been around the edge, were wonderfully brown and the chicken was perfectly cooked. Our guest produced some rounds of *shrak* bread which his mother had made. We tore them into pieces and used them to pick up our mouthfuls from the hot platter. It was wonderful.

We then made a different fire and boiled a pot of water on three stones to make bedouin tea. Sugar and herbs are added to the water. Finally, when it has reached boiling point, the tea is added. This was usually loose tea but we sometimes had to use tea-bags. Once cooled, these were Azuz's favourite treats; the bag itself and the Lipton's label. After drinking a couple of glasses of tea, our guest just got up and wandered off, without any thanks and with no formal or even detectable leave-taking. This surprised me at the time but I learned that this was not unusual. Much is made of greetings, welcoming friends or strangers to your home or your camp fire. Leave-taking is nothing. No eye contact. Nothing.

The journey back took longer than two hours, because we returned by a more difficult, but very beautiful route that brought us into an enclosed wadi behind Little Petra [thought by some to have been the original Nabbatean city centre before the flourishing trade of providing water and hospitality at this crossing of caravan routes brought greater wealth and the need for the finer city known as Petra.] The Nabbateans had created a successful, prosperous community here. The Romans left them in peace for many years but then, in AD 116, jealous of the Nabbatean wealth and influence, the Romans forcibly diverted the caravan routes to by-pass Petra. The Nabbatean civilisation never recovered. This and subsequent devastating earthquakes were the reasons that Petra lay unknown to the outside world for nearly two thousand years.

The enclosed wadi was a wonderful, natural defence. At one point, the excellent Azuz baulked at being expected to cross the narrow ledge that lay before us. There were a lot of encouraging clicks from Bassam but Azuz simply didn't like the look of it. Bassam asked me to dismount and to go ahead, on foot. Indeed, it was almost too much for me. The ledge was twenty feet long and really very narrow. To the left was the smooth, vertical rock face. To the right was a sheer ten-foot drop. Azuz watched most carefully. My carefree performance should have earned me an Equity card. I turned and said,

"Come on, old fellow. It's all right." Having seen that it could be done, that wonderful donkey bravely and steadily crossed to safety. It was adventures such as this that consolidated the mutual trust between Bassam, Azuz and me.

Chapter 4
Thraya's Story

One of our favourite destinations for a day's ride was *Jebel Haroun,* The Mount of Aaron. This is the highest mountain in Petra and was reputedly the last resting place of Aaron, the brother of Moses. Having fled from Egypt and, in search of the Promised Land, the Children of Israel traversed this region, the ancient land of Edom. There are many biblical references to their presence here; Mount Sela, the copper mines in Wadi Araba and, most notably, Mount Nebo, further north in the land of Moab- whence Moses looked out and saw the Promised Land. I always felt a great sense of history; that I was walking or riding on paths that many had trod before me. Pieces of broken pottery littered the ground in places. In others ancient stairways, carved from the solid rock and worn smooth from years of use and erosion, stood as testament to the lives that had been lived here for so many years.

Jebel Haroun is revered by Christians and Muslims alike. At the summit is a small, white-domed church marking the site where Aaron is thought to have been buried. Legend has it that, in the seventh century, the future Prophet Mohammed as a boy, accompanied by his uncle, made a pilgrimage here. The Christian guardian of the tomb looked at the boy and said:

"You will change the world."

The journey to *Jebel Haroun* takes one and half hours on donkey back from the centre of Petra. The twin-peaked mountain dominates the skyline and towers over the southern approaches to the ancient city centre. When our rides took us in this direction, I used to meet Bassam in Petra itself. I would buy a ticket at the gate in Wadi Musa and walk down through the outer siq followed by the narrow siq itself. This natural cleft in the mountains, whose rock faces range from 300-600 feet in height and where chariot-worn cobbles can still be seen, provided an excellent, defensive approach to the city. Emerging from the siq, the tourist comes face to face with *Al Khazneh,* The Treasury, the best preserved and best known of the Rose Red City's facades.

The Treasury is about two kilometres from the city centre where the Bedouin men ply their trade.

"Do you want a ride? It is better to ride. Look! My donkey is air-conditioned."

To save time and effort before the long ride, Bassam didn't come to meet me. He simply sent Azuz. He would point him in the right direction, slap his hind quarters and shout "*Harwah!* Go." I would look out for him on the way and, when I saw him, call,

"*Azuz ta'al.* Azuz, come here." He would immediately approach, turn and wait to be mounted. I should say that he waited for me to lead him to a big boulder so that I could climb up in order to mount him. I freely confess to a heart that swelled with pride, knowing the effect that this sight was having on the local men, as they watched from their souvenir shops or camel backs or paused in their talks to the groups of tourists.

Thraya's cave.

Twenty minutes along the dusty track to *Jebel Haroun*, in an area called *Hamdooda,* lived Bassam's half-sister, Thraya. Her home is a former tomb. The main chamber is about twelve feet square with a raised platform to the right, where the bodies would have been placed, and a smaller recess in the facing wall of unknown purpose. At that time, Thraya was living there with ten of her eleven children whose ages ranged from four to eighteen years. She and Bassam shared the same father, Ali.

Thraya was then in her forties. She was, and is, a fine looking woman. Unlike many of the other women, who wear straight black fustans with long sleeves and rounded necks, she preferred to wear the *madraga* – a sleeveless, V-

25

necked long pinafore dress, worn over a long-sleeved blouse.

By the time she was fifteen her mother, who had been Ali's second wife, was dead, leaving her and her younger brother Sa'ood motherless. Her father was in his fifties at this time. He had divorced his first wife, his second wife was dead and he needed another. His eye fell upon H'layla, a lovely 15 year old. Her family was sympathetic to the idea of the match, but didn't want to deplete their 'stock' of marriageable girls.

"You can have H'layla," they said, "but we want to trade her for your 15 year old daughter, Thraya." And so it was that Thraya married into H'layla's family, and Ali won his young bride. H'layla's marriage to Ali was long and very successful. When he died six years ago, he was the oldest man in the village. H'layla bore him eight children, two daughters and six sons, one of whom is my splendid guide, Bassam.

Thraya was not so lucky. For some years, she lived in harmony with her husband and the second wife he took fairly soon after their marriage. Their home was one of the best tomb sites on the Wadi Sabra side of Petra. It was substantial, with one major triclinium, a three-sided dining room, and several side rooms, including a kitchen and a Nabbatean cistern to catch the rain water. Then, with the coming of the tourists, the site was cleared and they all moved to one of the breeze block units in the village.

Shortly after the move, her husband took a third, sixteen year old wife, built an extension to his home for her and their family and from then on lived almost exclusively with her. Thraya became very unhappy and returned with her children to *Hamdooda* and to the poorer tomb that she was living in when I first met her. Her life was very hard. Away from the village, she received less support from her husband. This was particularly felt at *Eid*, the celebration that marks the end of Ramadan. At this time, the children always have new outfits. For many years, her children could only look with envy at the new things being sported by the other children.

Her brother and half-brothers helped her from time to time, but she still had to make necklaces from melon seeds, in the hope that she could sell them to passing tourists. Her extended family belonged to a group called the Samaheen. They did not allow their women to work at Petra, exposed to the tourists. They preferred their wives and daughters to be either at home or in the mountains tending the family goats. In circumstances such as this, however, when the alternative was having to provide more money from their own pockets, the rules were bent and Thraya was allowed to ply her meagre trade.

Shrak at Thraya's

Despite her poverty, she was always very quick to invite me to her home. In later years when I was living in the village, I usually went for Friday lunch. On Fridays, the Sabbath, most of the tourists are Jordanian, wanting to view their heritage on their only day off. The chances of selling a necklace on a Friday were absolutely nil. The walk from Um Sayhoun to her cave took an hour and a half and involved a descent of 500 feet down into Petra and a climb up out of about 300 feet. There is no shade at any point on that track. It was a punishing journey but one that her school-age children made five days a week.

Thraya made the most wonderful bread. A wood fire would be burning as she kneaded the dough. When ready it was placed on a metal sheet, then flattened and shaped to the sides. Embers and ash from the fire were placed directly onto the dough. Then it was put to one side for about fifteen minutes. When it was ready, Thraya would strike the sheet on the bare rock, turn the bread upside down, give it some knocks and there it was - delicious food with not a speck of ash to spoil the taste.

She used to visit me often when she came to the village. One day she arrived with her four- year-old grand-daughter. She asked me if I had some more pain killers, like the ones I had given her sister-in-law. This was the most common medicinal need among the women. I always returned from visits home to England, having bought a supply for my neighbours. They had so much more faith in foreign tablets. They were much stronger than Jordanian ones, they said.

"Fee haboob? Have you got any tablets?" was one of the first questions I learned to understand in Arabic. So, I cut four tablets from their foil and offered them to her. Thraya took them but they were not what she wanted. A linguistic pantomime followed. She held out her index

finger and held the base of it with the fingers of her other hand. She then indicated a pain in her lower back. Unfortunately, but not surprisingly, I thought that she was asking me for suppositories. I have no idea whether she realised what I was thinking, or whether she understood the look on my face before the penny dropped and I worked out that she was trying to indicate that she wanted a little bottle of *haboob* for back pain. I promised to bring some back with me on my next visit to England.

She then lifted up the skirt of her *madraga*, rolled up one of her leggings and revealed varicose veins which had caused puffiness behind her right knee. She had to walk a lot. Her donkey had died and there was no money for a replacement. Her shoes were the cheapest sort of black moulded plastic slip-ons. She was clearly in a lot of pain. As she showed me her knee, I saw that there was very little material left in the soles of her socks. She kept pulling them round her foot to disguise their state. I made Bedouin tea with *gurfa,* cinnamon, and offered her some biscuits. She was clearly tired, so she settled on the mattress with her grand-daughter and I sat quietly by while she slept.

When she awoke, I brought out my bag of socks. She took two pairs of new, 100% cotton . In the bottom of my wardrobe was an unpacked bag of shoes of various kinds. All were judged to be "*Kwai –ez.* Good". I was happy to let her take them.

As the years went on and Thraya's older sons married, her circumstances became less desperate, as they contributed to the living expenses of their mother and their siblings. I twice drove her to visit hospitals in Amman; once to keep an appointment for her 14 year old daughter who was born with a noticeable cast in her eye. Thraya's husband had been in the army. His family were therefore entitled to free care at the military hospital. One of her sons came with us. Three years later, the surgeons successfully operated on her daughter's eye. Within six months, someone came for her and within a year, she was married.

The second occasion, this time chaperoned by a different son, was for Thraya herself. She was keen to visit a particular hospital about which she had heard good reports, but she needed two hundred dinars. [At that time, about £150.] I lent it to her. She was never able to repay it but often apologised that the debt was still outstanding.

She was seen by the doctor almost immediately and was then insistent that we should return home directly. She was twenty years my junior. I had driven for three hours and, after only thirty minutes, she wanted me to drive back. Everything about her spoke of her country origins and poverty. The city was no place for her. I therefore agreed to set off on the return journey. At the half-way point, we stopped at a rudimentary resting place. Her son bought tea and a piece of bread rolled around a Kraft cheese triangle. Thraya smoked roll-up cigarettes. Some said it was *heeshee,* a kind of pot. Whatever it was, the mix contained goat droppings and the smell was foul. I didn't let Thraya smoke in the car, so she was desperate. While her son was making his purchases and, not wanting to smoke in public, Thraya found a convenient small, carpeted room in which to light up. Her son was immediately summoned from the queue by the owner of the cafe in order to control his mother. Her smoking room of choice was, in fact, the men's prayer room. Yes. There was a certain eccentricity about Thraya.

On another occasion, Thraya and I were lunch guests of Bassam and his wife, Fatma, whose home was above mine. I was exhausted after a long ride and was grateful for the invitation. Other guests included two of Thraya's children, Fatma's mother, two of Fatma's seven sisters and three of their children. After the meal, I slipped away, with thanks, needing a shower and a doze in the heat of the day. However, Thraya followed me home and settled herself onto a mattress in the sunny hall. She was coughing a lot and showed me four different boxes of tablets. She then started to roll one of her cigarettes.

"Hathee mush fucket kwai-ez. That is not a good idea," I told her. "Would she like some pineapple juice instead?" She did not recognise the Arabic word for "pineapple", so I brought the juice from the fridge to show her the picture of the fruit on the carton. That image, too, was unknown to her. She unscrewed the top, smelled the contents and promptly began to drink directly from the carton. When she had finished, I returned the juice to the fridge, hoping fervently that the temperature of the fridge was sufficient to kill any bugs left on the spout.

About a year later, on another of her visits to the village, Thraya appeared on my doorstep. She was wearing a colourful, new headscarf and wanted me to drive her to Ma'an. This the regional capital, some half hour's drive away.

"Why do you want to go there?" I asked. She would have to pay. Maybe she had sold some jewellery to the tourists, maybe one of her sons, or half-brothers, had given her money.

"There is a good lady doctor there", she had heard. I had already taken, at different times, two other neighbours to an excellent Iraqi doctor in Ma'an. I remembered the location of the surgery so, thinking that we were talking about the same doctor, I agreed to drive her. The journey from Um Sayhoun to Ma'an was across an exposed, barren plateau with no trees along the route to provide any shade from the fierce sun.

The approach to the town centre took us down a street lined with greengrocers. The road here was dual carriageway, albeit with a single narrow lane in each direction, separated by quite a wide central reservation. There were many people on the street, mostly men doing the family shopping, so I was driving at about 15 kph. I could see that a man was crossing the road. By his long beard and his white skull-cap, I could tell that he was an elder from a mosque, maybe even an Imam. He was on the central reservation and, being aware of the approach of my car, was slowing down to stop at the curb. At that point, he lifted his eyes, saw that we were two women in the car, and deliberately stepped right in front of the car. I stood on the brakes and stopped eight feet from him. He reached the other curb. I didn't move. I waited for his backward glance of triumph, and I wasn't disappointed. What a wonderful point he thought that he had scored.

As we neared what I thought was our destination, Thraya began to say,

"We need to stop and ask the way."

"Why?" I replied. "I know the way. I have brought both Airlia and Fatma to the same Iraqi lady doctor."

"No.No," said Thraya. "I want the *hujamah*".

"What's that?" I asked.

"It's a kind of hospital", she said. We stopped and asked a man who gave us directions to where he thought it was. We could see nothing resembling anything apparently medical. So, I then stopped and asked a lady, thinking that it was a destination more likely to be known by a woman. She paused briefly as I wound the window down. She was afraid. She could see that we were two women needing help. Her greater concern was for the onlookers, who might not be able to see that the occupants of the car were female.

She didn't want to be reported to her husband or family as having been seen speaking to someone in a car.

We had more luck with the next man.

"Oh," he said. "You are on the wrong side of the town. It is over by the Electricity Board offices." We had in fact passed it on our way to the town centre. I parked by the offices and one more enquiry helped us pinpoint the *hujamah*.

It was the front room of someone's private home. Two ladies welcomed us. This was something new, they thought, a foreigner and a Bedouin.

"Ah," they said to me, "you are beautifully dressed. *Inti Muslima?* Are you a Muslim?" I was indeed wearing a traditional *fustan* and my head was almost covered with a scarf. I chose to dress like this in order to identify with the women I was helping, but I always left some hair visible at the front.

"Do sit down," they said. So I sat, and Thraya sat six feet away, facing me. The ladies went and stood behind her, near a table on which there appeared to be pieces of equipment resembling oxygen masks. Thraya removed her headscarf and the black balaclava-type cap that concealed her side hair. The fastenings on the back of her *madraga* were loosened and the back of her neck and shoulders laid bare.

One of the ladies then began to apparently pinch various places on Thraya's back. Each time a paroxysm of pain crossed her face. It was only then that I noticed that the lady had a razor blade in her hand. The second lady was mopping up the blood which flowed from the wounds. When the ladies were happy that there were enough wounds, they took one of the 'oxygen masks', applied it to Thraya's back and then pumped it in order first, to create a vacuum and then to draw blood from the wounds. As each suction pump, containing what looked to me like considerable amounts of very dark-coloured blood, was emptied out, another was put on an adjacent area. Throughout, the women hardly addressed a word to Thraya. They were more interested in me.

"Ah. You are not a Muslim? It is better to be Muslim. There is only one straight path. All must follow it."

Eventually, all was done and Thraya's dress was put in order. She produced the money that the ladies asked for. I felt great relief. If she had wanted to borrow from me - a not unreasonable possibility given our history – I would have had to refuse. What I had witnessed seemed to me to be a particularly barbaric form of blood-letting. However, it was clearly popular. We had had to wait while another client was dealt with and there were two more ladies waiting after Thraya. On the way home, I asked,

"Why did you want to come here? What is wrong with you?"

"Ah," she said. "I keep having terrible headaches."

The following week, I met her on the street.

"How are your headaches?" I asked.

"Oh.....they were much better for a while but they are starting to come back."

"Well, please do not ask me to take you to a *hujamah* again!"

Chapter 5
Al Barra

Al Barra is a craggy mountain, lying between *Um Al Biyara,* The Mother of Cisterns, and *Jebel haroun.* It became one of my favourite destinations, but not until I had earned its respect. I am quite sure that the mountain tested me, checking to see if I were worthy to set foot on its slopes.

It set me three tests. The first was the most challenging. Access to the mountain is by no means easy. Small cairns were strategically placed to indicate the best tracks. One of the main approaches involved turning right off the track very close to Thraya's cave. We needed to dismount and lead the donkeys up through a rock-strewn, narrow ravine which apparently guarded the entrance to the mountain from this side. We re-mounted and were soon riding across a small plateau. It was very inhospitable terrain. Having been struck by that thought, I noticed an old man approaching on foot, with a long stick in his hand, serving as a shepherd's crook. I followed Bassam's lead and dismounted. He knew this old man. His name was Salaama and he was Fatma's grandfather. No one knew his exact age but all agreed that he was over 100 years. Bassam introduced me.

"Hi Joanna. Heeya min Samaheen. This is Joanna. She is from the Samaheen," their tribal sub-group. Smiles and a handshake. Bassam was speaking very loudly. Clearly Salaama was hard of hearing. After a few brief words, he went on his way to find his goats. Shortly after, we passed a beautifully symmetrical Juniper tree.

"That's Salaama's home," Bassam said. I looked and saw that, hanging from a the tree, were several plastic bags containing the old man's meagre belongings, alongside cooking pots and tea kettles. There was no sign of the usual thin sleeping mattress. He probably slept in favourite hollows in the compacted earth. Salaama could have lived with any of his children in the village but this was the life he wanted, alone on this mountain, his goats his only company.

Ahead of us appeared an apparently impenetrable rock face. Bassam explained that I needed to go on alone, on foot, while he led the donkeys on another route, higher up. He indicated a narrow cleft in the rock and said,

"Just keep going straight."

I felt considerable trepidation but I did what he said. The sound of the animals hooves quickly ceased and, there I was, alone on this rugged mountain. The cleft I had to negotiate was full of rocks which, over millennia, had tumbled from on high to this place. Just discernible was a faint track where others had walked before, leading up into the cleft. At one point I had to squeeze between two huge boulders; a place so narrow that I couldn't remain upright.

Having emerged from that obstacle course, I had to walk onto a ledge in the rock face with a considerable drop to my right. Bassam had said, "Straight on." Well, so far, there had been absolutely no choice of route. Thereafter I just tried to keep walking straight, an impossible task given the matrix of small steep wadis that criss-crossed the route.

After about half an hour, I reached a wide flat area which led to the mountain's edge. I could see *Jebel Haroon* across the very deep wadi which separated the two mountains.

"I've done it!" I thought. "This is my land. It recognises me and is being kind to me." After a further twenty minutes, I was standing on the edge, but nowhere could I see Bassam. I sat in the shade of a rock and recovered from what had been a difficult walk in a temperature of maybe 28 degrees. After a while with still no sign of Bassam, I clambered up onto the rock which had provided the shade. My eyes swept the mountain in both directions, but still nothing. Then I heard a call and saw a waving hand.

"Keep calling please," I shouted. I knew that after I had climbed down from the rock, Bassam would be out of sight. There were at least two dips in the land between us. By the time that I reached him, the tea pot was ready, another wonderful *casteer* [the foil parcel of chicken and vegetables] was being prepared and the donkeys were happily grazing. The donkey-friendly route he had taken had been blocked. He had retraced our steps, gone around the bottom of the mountain and had climbed up the steep side which we were overlooking.

Unlike many of the men, Bassam was very good at making eye contact when being spoken to. This time he was different. He didn't know where to put his eyes. Then I realised the cause. With all the effort in that heat, I had removed my long-sleeved shirt and had tied the arms around my waist. Beneath it, I was wearing a short-sleeved T-shirt. The sight of my bare forearms, alone, as we were in that place, was an embarrassing difficulty for him. I pretended that the wind had cooled me down and I replaced my shirt.

It was just as well because, over the next hour, that desolate place became a veritable Piccadilly Circus. First a young woman of about 15 years and her six-year old brother appeared. They were looking after a herd of goats. She was very shy and had her face fully covered at first. Then, when she saw that I was a woman and realised too that she knew Bassam's family, she uncovered her face. We invited them to stay and have lunch. The little boy amused himself by using a chalky piece of rock to draw on the bed rock.

Then two men appeared in the distance, one riding a donkey. They joined us – just as the meal was ready. They were travelling from one encampment to another. We all sat on the rocks, enjoying the food, especially the little boy who was clearly very hungry.

After we had finished, we made another pot of tea. While we were drinking that, a woman appeared at the fire. She had just climbed up the mountain with a baby on her back, slung in a cloth bag, the handles of which were stretched across the mother's forehead. She looked very tired. Her baby started crying, so she quite naturally started breast-feeding. Then a boy of about 14 years appeared. He was her son, but she had been faster than him in climbing up the mountain.

At that point, I realised that one of the two men with the donkey had disappeared. I asked Bassam and he said that he would explain later. We cleared everything up, leaving left-over food for the mountain animals. The only thing that Azuz was interested in, as usual, was the used tea bags.

We started our journey back and Bassam explained about the missing man. He was the older son of the woman with the baby. He worked away from home and had told his mother that he had to work that weekend and couldn't come home. So, when he recognised his mother climbing up the mountain, he had set off quickly in the opposite direction!

We were going to return down the steep mountainside in front of us. It had no craggy patches but was covered with shale. I mounted Azuz and we set off. I was in the habit of not using stirrups. In the early days, when I first started riding, I had developed pains in my shins from the unnatural angle at which the stirrups held my legs. We were about a third of the way down, when one of Azuz's front hooves slipped on a piece of shale. He quickly regained his footing but, without the stirrups, I slipped off the left-hand side of him, hit my back on the only visible boulder and slithered to the ground under him. Bassam was at my side immediately. I was thoroughly winded and needed to lie a while.

Azuz had stopped dead in his tracks for fear of treading on me. Despite the pain, the uncomfortable proximity of Azuz's black penis, which was dangling eight inches from my face, was not lost on me. I eventually managed to rise and to re-mount. Bassam said,

"You must use the stirrups!" So I did. We made it back to the village without further incident and Bassam then drove me back to my hotel. After a very uncomfortable night, I drove back to Amman and, as I was entering my apartment block, I met the lady whose family owns the building. She invited me to tea. Her husband was there too. He was an eminent chest/lung specialist. After talking for a while, I mentioned my sore ribs. He examined me – almost over the tea cups - and sent me to the hospital where one of his sons was on duty in casualty. The X-ray revealed a fractured number 10 rib. I was given a pain-killing injection and sent home with the X-rays to show my landlord. He said,

"The rib is not just fractured. The two pieces are totally disconnected." The pain was so great for about two weeks that it took all of my energy to perform essential daily tasks, including going to school and teaching. After that I was back on the same donkey, having earned the respect of both Azuz and Bassam.

The second test occurred a couple of months later when we were making a new approach to the mountain via a sandy wadi. The vegetation here was lush, with white oleanders overhanging the track. Azuz walked on purposefully, knowing where he was going. He didn't have a problem. The oleanders weren't at his eye level. They were at mine. Up went my hands to brush the branches away. Unfortunately, these were mature branches which did not easily give way and I stupidly held on. Unaware that I could be so silly, Azuz kept walking, causing me to slip off his back, letting go of the branches and landing ignominiously on the ground. Not for me a soft, sandy landing. No. There just happened to be a stone the size of a grapefruit where my left thigh landed. To this day, I have an indentation in the soft tissue on that leg.

The final trial involved my slipping onto a fierce thorn bush. We were following a narrow goat track down a steep bank, on foot. I lost my footing and sat down heavily on a dry, low shrub whose needle-like thorns were an inch to an inch and a half long. The pain was excruciating, as if each tip had been dipped in deadly poison. Bassam was several yards ahead of me. He gallantly climbed back up and, having previously been embarrassed by the sight of my forearms, had no trouble extracting the offending needles from my backside.

There was no doubt in my mind that this mountain was guarding its privacy; not only for its own sake, but also for that lovely old man, Salaama.

Chapter 6
My First Ramadan

In 2004, Ramadan was thirty days over October and November. The exact start and end of Ramadan are eagerly awaited by all. It is a question of the "Wise Men" scrutinizing the night sky and studying the state and visibility of the moon. The end of Ramadan was strange that year. In Saudi Arabia, Pakistan, Syria and the West Bank, Ramadan ended on 12th November. In Jordan, however, there was cloud and the new moon had not been visible. Ramadan therefore lasted an extra day, until the 13th.

It is a strange time. It seems that the whole population observes the daylight fasting, whether or not they are regular worshippers. Families rise at 4am, eat a heavy meal of something like pasta, then go back to bed. The working day starts, and ends, earlier. People in Amman start to return to their homes between one and two in the afternoon in order to rest and pray before *iftar*, the meal which breaks the fast, at approximately six o'clock.

It is not a time at which to be on the road. It is a rush hour like no other. In the daylight hours, the faithful abstain from eating, drinking, nicotine, medicines and sexual activity. So, not only are drivers hungry, they are desperate for a cigarette and the tension shows in their driving. With cigarettes as cheap as 75 pence for a packet of twenty, smoking is very common indeed, particularly among the men. It does not have the same social stigma that it has acquired in the West and the dangers of passive smoking seem to be unknown. The tiniest of children are forced to inhale cigarette smoke in crowded cars, small family rooms and in the arms of those holding them.

I have seen sections of road, particularly at the approach to traffic lights, changed from three lanes into six or seven lanes as drivers mount the curb or leave absolutely no room between the lines of cars – all desperate to cross at the next green signal. Indeed, I have not only seen it but have also been trapped in it. On Thursdays, to get safely away from Amman and to head south was a great relief. Members of the family took it in turns to provide the *iftar* meal. I particularly remember my first *iftar* at the home of H'layla and Ali, Bassam's parents. Ali, at this time, was somewhere between 95 and 100 years old, still with all his faculties, albeit physically frail.

Most of his sons and their wives had spent several hours preparing the meal. The men slaughter, skin and butcher the goats, usually from their own herd. The women prepare the shrak bread on open fires, soak the rice, painstakingly pick fresh coriander leaves from the stalks for garnish, fry peanuts for the same purpose and prepare *salat arabi*. This consists of tomato and cucumber, cubed, with added salt and lemon juice. The women always prepare food while seated cross-legged on the floor. Chopping boards are unknown. They hold their hands over a plastic bowl and very dextrously slice the vegetables; first with a matrix of vertical slices, then the horizontal slices that send the cubes tumbling into the bowl.

I was among the first to arrive, other than the family members who had been preparing the meal. The yard was neat and all prepared; thin mattresses formed three sides of a square with cushions for reclining. The men would dine here. Ali was sitting alone waiting for his guests. He greeted me warmly and invited me to sit beside him. His hearing was remarkably good for so old a man. Conscious that I had not been welcomed by H'layla, who was busy indoors, I went in search of her. She was busy counting the *shrak* to ensure that she had enough. There must have been about thirty rounds of bread, each approximately 18-20" in diameter.

A white plastic chair was brought for me, but the women were busy moving around me, so I returned to Ali. After a few minutes, one of his sons and another man arrived and sat down. That was the unspoken signal for me to leave that space to the men and to return indoors. Things were gaining pace there. Fatma, Bassam's wife, indicated a mattress for me to sit on, thoughtfully selected with a wall behind for me to lean on. I was immediately given a lovely two-month old baby girl to hold. She was Yasmine, one of H'layla's grandchildren. She was wrapped papoose-style and was fast asleep in a light soft carrying bag. Two younger sisters of H'layla arrived, one with a young baby which she started to breast-feed almost as soon as she had sat down. Within five minutes, three little girls came and sat by me. They were aged from seven to eleven years. Was I Bassam's second wife? Where was my husband? Did I have any children? How old was my son? Was he married? How old was I? Where was I from?

One had a torn piece of file paper in the hand. I asked her what it was and she indicated that it was a fan for her face. I asked to borrow it and made neat, concertina-like folds. She was delighted to see the effect when I released the folds and she went off to show everyone. In the meantime, women old and young arrived. I knew most of them, at least by sight. There must have been about fifteen women and an equal number of children, all in the one room. From my place I could see that the courtyard had filled. There were maybe fifteen to twenty men there. Some were dressed in western clothes but most were traditionally dressed in *thawbs,* the long, straight gowns, and red and white *keffiyehs*, wrapped in various styles about their heads.

The eagerly-awaited call that the sun had set was made from the mosque's public address system. Immediately, dates and juice were served. Also, from the fridge, came *shaneena*, a runny, delicious, unsweetened goats' milk yoghurt. A few minutes later Ali, wondering where his meal was, came in with his prayer mat under his arm, looking for H'layla. R'Kheeya, Bassam's youngest sister, recently married to Ahmad a tourist policeman in Aqaba, marshalled the children into a separate room. One little girl sitting close beside me was reluctant to leave and was allowed to stay.

Her mother, Ayeesha, aged twenty six and a cousin of Bassam, had died two months previously. She had been at home, alone with her five children, when she fell to the floor, unconscious. According to the villagers, she was taken to hospital and was seen by someone who, knowing that she was from the *b'dool* [the poor Bedouin of Um Sayhoun] and assuming that such people lived in filth, deduced that she was suffering from food poisoning and admitted her to hospital. Three days later, a consultant from Amman arrived. He requested a scan and discovered that she had suffered a cerebral haemorrhage. She died two weeks later, having failed to regain consciousness, on the day when her youngest child was forty days old. Ayeesha's mother was her father's first wife. He had another, much younger wife who was herself breast-feeding a child. So, the baby's step-grandmother became the child's wet nurse.

In anticipation of the arrival of the *mansaf,* plastic table cloths from a perforated roll, were spread on the floor. With the children gone, the women could form themselves into circles, ready for the large shallow platters of food. Soon after, we could see the first steaming platter being carried out to the men. A second followed, also for the men. Our platter was the third. We were honoured; the boiled, bleached skull of one of the goats took pride of place in the centre of the rice. All the soft tissue was distributed on the rice and covered in yoghurt sauce. The brown teeth were still in its jawbone, looking for all the world as if they were ready to tuck into their own flesh.

Fatma was in my group and she could see that I was struggling to eat with my hands. In fact, in the face of the goat, I was struggling to eat at all. A spoon was sent for and all should have been well. I needed to rest my left hand on the floor while I was eating, so I had to be adept with the spoon. The most difficult thing to do one-handed is to cut a piece of meat off the bone. The old woman to my right, seeing my difficulty, kept my triangular wedge of the platter supplied with choice pieces of lean meat. To my left, a teenage girl was concentrating on sucking every last bit of goodness from the marrow of one of the bones; tapping the bone on the floor and then sucking again.

The only sour note of the evening was struck by Zaynab, Fatma's oldest sister and the mother of the afflicted boy who featured in the incident in chapter one. She had a reputation for being rather cantankerous. In addition, she was newly returned from the hajj [the pilgrimage to Mecca] and was feeling very self-righteous in her distinctive all-black apparel. In order to eat, she had to lift the black flap on her facial covering. She now took exception to the fact that the front half of my feet were visible. All shoes had been left at the door, so the issue was the feet themselves which, despite the temperature, were already covered in opaque black tights. In this society, in these circumstances, I was being rude. No other woman in the room minded, understanding the difficulty I was in. Fortunately, I was wearing a traditional Bedouin dress, with my head covered, and I was just able to pull the skirt material down far enough to conceal the offending toes.

Despite my misgivings about the skeletal head, the meal was truly delicious. Sometimes, if the fire has been too strong and the meat has been boiled too quickly, it can have a cloyingly rich taste, but this was cooked to perfection. As I sat back to indicate that I had finished eating and spoke the words *hamdu lillah,* thank God, all in my circle encouraged me to eat more. When I told them that I was satisfied, they continued to eat, quietly and efficiently cleaning the platter with their fingers, happy in the knowledge that I wanted nothing more.

Towards the end of the meal, a group of three or four boys who had been eating with the men, came and fought over our goat's head. I later saw one of the boys with the head tucked under his arm, running his finger around the eye socket in order to capture the last vestiges of some unspeakable delicacy.

The bones and other debris were removed, some women left, the plastic cloths were gathered up and the floor was swept. Just then a bonny little girl of about 15 months approached. She was brandishing a 5-6 inch bone, heavy with meat. She attacked it with all the ferocity of a lion enjoying its kill. I saw her again about 20 minutes later and the bone was almost picked clean.

Sweetened tea in small glasses was then served. It was delicious. Just what my palate needed. I rose – not without difficulty – took my leave of H'layla and Ali and left. My distaste for the sight of the food and my fear of eating unrecognised offal, were made bearable by my utter delight in the women. They are lovely. They are kind and sensitive. They are welcoming and accepting. They have, on average, eight children each. They are old before their time. Their teeth are weakened after repeated breast-feeding. They are the salt of the earth and I love them.

Chapter 7
Bassam's Story

Bassam is quite simply the best 'donkey-man' in Petra. He is hard-working, his animals are well fed and happy, he knows the mountains like the back of his hand, he speaks very good English and he is very sensitive to the varied needs of the tourists who trust him and his animals.

On my first visit to Petra, I had ridden up to *Al Deir,* the monastery, on a donkey owned by a Bassam Ali. He was a good man; very kind with his novice rider and, on that day, elated by the birth of a new child. On my return six weeks later, I asked among the Bedouin for the same man. A man approached and said that he was Bassam Ali. I wasn't certain that it was the same man, but he looked 'right' so I engaged him to take me to *Jebel Haroun* and *Wadi Sabra.* We had a wonderful day. He anticipated every potential worry that I might have, helping me to gain confidence and to enjoy this wonderful land, off the beaten track. On our return from the ride, another man was waiting for us at the donkey station.

"I am Bassam Ali," he said. Indeed he was. He was Bassam Ali Salaama and my new guide was Bassam Ali Bassam. The two men were first cousins. Both their fathers were called Ali. The name of one *grand*father, however, was Salaama and the name of the other was Bassam. In later years, it made perfect sense to me, when official forms required the applicant to name fathers and grandfathers. Bassam Ali Salaama was very good-natured about the confusion. Shortly afterwards, he turned his attention from donkeys to selling jewellery and always greeted me warmly when our paths crossed.

That day marked the start of a wonderful friendship between Bassam Ali Bassam and me. Every weekend I spent Friday and Saturday in the mountains on Azuz. There was not a peak that our wonderful animals couldn't manage. In fact, they knew every track. If the track forked, they just needed to know that day's destination. Sometimes, depending on the mood he was in, Azuz liked to go fast, sometimes slowly. A gentle kick from me was often enough. Very occasionally he would simply stop, and then ignore the kick. I soon realised that, on these occasions, he was lightening the load on his bowels. The sweet smell would drift up to my nostrils. Then, when he had finished, he would turn right around so that he could smell and admire his handiwork.

On other occasions, the scent of a female donkey would reach his nostrils. He would produce a deafening racket, hee-hawing this way and that. He couldn't bray and walk at the same time. It was very amusing. When he was coming to the end of the calling, he didn't just stop suddenly. He wound down, as it were, ending with a most satisfying grunt or sigh. I usually said to him,

"Do you feel better now?"

In those early days, while I was still learning to ride, Bassam walked everywhere; always ready to help me, should the need arise. One day we were climbing to the top of a pretty high mountain. The earth was so barren that not even the goats had left tracks. So we had to pick our way very carefully. Two thirds of the way up the boulder-strewn slope, I had to dismount and proceed on foot. The view from the top was wonderful. We could see for miles, right over Wadi Araba into Israel. There was a lot of good firewood up there too, so we made the fire, prepared *casteer* and then rested for the hour that it took to cook.

While we were eating, Azuz was grazing on some clumps of herb nearby. When we had finished and wanted to leave, he was nowhere to be seen. Bassam had to carry the saddlebags and I took the saddle blankets which he had taken from the donkey for me to sit on. We called as we went. Three quarters of the way down the mountain, we emerged from a rocky wadi and saw him. Had he stopped because he had heard us calling? No. Had he stopped to wait for us? No. He had stopped because a big knot in his rein had caught between two rocks. What a donkey.

One month later, in March 2005, he died. He was twelve years old. He might have lived until he was twenty. The day before, he had been strong. He had been happy, rolling in the soft wadi sand. That night, he wasn't hungry. In the morning, I rode him for the last time. His step was slow. His breathing changed. We reached the donkey station. Bassam led him to a cave. Azuz lay down and lost consciousness. The Brooke Hospital vet was called. He gave him an injection to try to stimulate his heart, but he could not help him. An hour later he died.

Azuz was a king of donkeys; white, wise, sensitive, loyal and tolerant. When he spoke, he put his whole body into his voice. When he listened, his ears were omni-directional antennae. When an interesting smell hit his nostrils, he threw his head back, baring his teeth, to savour every scrap of it.

He taught me how he wanted to be ridden; up steep wadi sides, down rocky goat tracks, along tarmac roads. He answered the tugs on his single rein. Between his head and me was a cream crew-cut mane. How that mane had been my anchor when, stirrup-less by choice, we had made steep climbs!

Rosemary was his favourite herb. He would eat his way through the dry, tough outer twigs in order to get at the tender inner shoots. He ignored tasty left-overs like potatoes, onions and tomatoes in favour of used tea bags, complete with the 'Liptons' label.

Everyone wanted to ride him. Tour guides always looked for him. In recent months, on Fridays and Saturdays, they didn't find him. He was with me, in the mountains. We scaled every mountain-top in Petra. He was wonderful.

Bassam couldn't bear to be with him when he died. We took another donkey and, leaving Azuz with a friend, went up into the mountains. At that time, there were pockets of spring flowers adorning this drought-ridden land. My favourites were the red, small-headed poppies which produced wonderful splashes of colour on this monochrome landscape. Bassam's phone rang. Azuz had gone. We rode on in silence. I was crying. I didn't look around to see what Bassam was doing. Then he said,

"I will go and see him later."

"Please take some of these flowers and put them on his body," I said.

I don't know whether he ever did. I just know that Bassam waited with him until a winch lorry came to collect the carcass. Some weeks afterwards, when we were crossing a bridge over a steep narrow wadi, Bassam said,

"That is where they dropped Azuz."

It was shortly after this that Bassam felt sufficiently confident in my ability to ride, that he started riding himself, instead of walking alongside me. I noticed that he always rode behind me. At first I thought that he did this in order to see that all was well with me. Later I realised that it was an important signal to others that I was a client and that he was fulfilling the role of groom. Occasionally, if part of our ride took us onto the road, cars would blow their horns as they passed, with the male occupants shouting something unintelligible through the windows. I would say,

"Why did they do that?"

"Maybe they've never seen a woman on a donkey before," he said.

As my Arabic improved I realised that the passers-by weren't interested in whether or not I was a paying client. They saw one man with one woman and immediately assumed that the relationship must be intimate. Although I wore a headscarf in a traditional Bedouin way in order to protect myself from the sun, the wind, the cold and, indeed, to keep my hair out of my eyes, they could see that I was foreign. That could only mean one thing. My favours were available. Such behaviour usually came from passing motorists, but even Bassam's friends could not resist their own jokes when we came across them in the mountains. One day, a man on a camel approached. Bassam greeted him.

"How much do you want for her?" the stranger said.

"Ah......her skin is white, so I will want many camels," Bassam laughed back. I had understood. I said,

"*Wahad kelp.* Just one dog." They roared, but I was instinctively trying to make a point. Dogs are the most despised of animals. I wanted to match their joking tone, but I also wanted to indicate that the very idea behind the joke was not only ridiculous but was also offensive to me. There was a thirty-year age difference between Bassam and me, but that counted for nothing. Two years previously a twenty-five year old man from the village had married an Italian tourist and had gone to live with her in Italy. She was in her sixties and a grandmother. I started to notice subtle differences in Bassam's behaviour. In the mountains, alone, he was relaxed and his behaviour was at all times impeccable. Within sight of others, he became more distant.

At this time, Bassam was thirty years old. He was married to his first cousin, Fatma, and they had five children whose ages ranged from eleven to one year. Bassam's and Fatma's fathers were brothers but, fortunately, none of their children suffered from a congenital affliction. They had first met when they were ten, out tending their families' goats. At that first meeting, he had hit her with a stick. They were eighteen years old when they married.

Almost from the start of our friendship, we used to end our rides in the village. I was invited to their house for Bedouin tea or for a meal of *magloba*, a wonderful upside-down dish of chicken, rice, vegetables and spices. Fatma had been very uncertain of me at first. Who was this old English woman that her husband kept taking out? She was kind and welcoming but definitely wary, despite the fact that I was providing a steady income each weekend. The alternative for Bassam would have been the donkey station, hoping to attract passing tourists. I once asked Bassam if he thought that he would ever take a second wife.

"I do not know," was his reply. In his circle of family and friends, about a fifth of the men had two wives and two of his uncles had three.

Fatma might have been wary of me, but her children certainly weren't. On one of my first visits, her youngest son snatched my spectacles from my face and ran away with them.

"*La.La.* No. No," I cried. His older sister was more interested in returning them to me than was his mother. Spectacles were a novelty to him. With illiteracy rife in women over thirty, there was no need for them. In contrast, their night vision could easily beat any super-tech goggles.

Home for them and their five children was three bare rooms attached to his father's house. They had lived in one room until after the birth of their third child. Their first two children had been girls. On the birth of a son, a man is more often known as 'father of Faisal' or whatever the son's name is. Bassam was, unusually, known as *Abu Chofa*, the father of Chofa, named after his first-born daughter. At that time, the population of the village numbered about a thousand. Not then, nor at any time later, did I know of any other father who took the name of a daughter. In fact, Bassam had to withstand pressure from family and friends who urged him to change his name to *Abu Ahmad*, after his first son was born.

Fatma was, and is, very beautiful. There were, however, unusual features on her face. There was a slight mottling of the pigmentation of the skin and her eyelids were slightly tight. One day, Bassam explained what had happened. About a year before, Fatma had been at home with three of her children. The only heating was a calor gas fire on wheels. The second daughter Jasmine, then about ten, dragged the fire into the kitchen where her mother was working. Fatma had not heard the hiss of gas escaping from an unlit tap on the cooker. The combustion which resulted, blew the mother and daughter off their feet and burned both of their faces. Jasmine, who, being a little girl whose body was not entirely covered with clothes, suffered burns to her body too.

The first that Bassam heard was when a neighbour rode down to Petra to tell him that his father needed him at home. The man had kindly wanted to save the truth from Bassam for as long as possible. He left his work at once and began to ride up to the village. However, he crossed paths with some other men who called out:

"Your wife and daughter have been burnt in an explosion. They are taking them to hospital."

It was three days before either Fatma or Jasmine could open their eyes. Years later, Fatma confided to me that Bassam had cried at her bedside. In a society where any display of affection between man and wife, or indeed between anybody other than two men, is forbidden, his revelation of his feelings had been a source of great pride to her. She had the same kind of pride in her eyes when she also told me that, before they married, Bassam had told her that, if she ever dishonoured him, he would kill her. To her, this was a measure of how much he loved her.

Following the death of Azuz, I had started to ride Bassam's number two donkey. He was also white and called Aryam. He was the fastest donkey in Petra. During the first Gulf War when very few tourists came, the donkey men would amuse themselves by racing their donkeys between the Treasury and the donkey station at the bridge. Aryam always won. About two months after Azuz had died, in May or June of that year, we were returning from a ride and were on the outskirts of the village. I was in the lead, as usual, and trying to hold Aryam back because he knew that he was near his home and his wheat and hay. Suddenly a five or six- year old child who was sitting on the curb-side, did something which spooked the donkey. My peripheral vision had seen nothing. Aryam bucked. I rose and described a perfect parabola in the air until my head and right shoulder crunched into the gritty tarmac. The child melted from view and Bassam was by my side immediately, pouring water over my head.

I knew immediately that I had broken my collar bone because I could feel the bump. There was an egg-sized bump on the side of my head but this was nothing to what it could have been. My shoulder had saved me. Bassam and an elderly Bedouin man took me straight to the local hospital. The x-ray showed that the two sections of collar bone were overlapping each other by 3 centimetres. The doctors wanted me to return the next day to see the orthopaedic surgeon. Bassam, however, thought it best that I return directly to Amman. At that time, Bassam's car, like many of his neighbours', was an old white Nissan pick-up. His car had only two seats. It was out of the question that he should drive me, un-chaperoned, to Amman. However, Bassam's cousin had a four-seater. So he and his wife dropped everything they were doing and drove me to Amman, going as gently as they could over the thirty speed bumps which peppered the three-hour journey.

I telephoned ahead to one of my landlord's sons. As luck would have it, he was that very night, the doctor on duty in the local A and E department. He in turn phoned his father and arranged for him to wait up for me. We reached my apartment at eleven o'clock that night. Dr Khalil took one look at the x-ray and phoned the son on duty with instructions to admit me. Not only was my collar bone broken, but my shoulder blade was cracked.

"You've crushed the whole side of your thorax," he said.

My Bedouin friends were offered a bed for the night but they wouldn't stay. Another son, an orthodontist, drove me to the hospital where I spent two nights in a drugged sleep.

It was the following Autumn before I rode again. Thereafter, my mount of choice was one of Bassam's mules. I found that I preferred the rhythm of mule's gait. One day, we rode to somewhere very special. It was none of the peaks with their wonderful views and rock formations, but a place called *Wadi Nameer*. The entrance to the wadi is very narrow. Its portals are vertical rock faces. The floor of the wadi at that point is smooth bed-rock with an awkward climb over a rounded mound against the wall. Below the mound was one of those magical places where, after rain, the water lingers. The narrowness of the entrance meant that the sun could only reach this spot, in the late afternoon, for about half an hour each day.

After a while, the wadi opened up into a small apparently enclosed space. The ground was covered with soft sand and the rock faces towered in a circle above us. But then, around a corner, we came upon a flight of steps cut into the rock. I should say vestiges of steps. They must have been at least two thousand years old. The bottom ones had crumbled away and been replaced by loose rocks. The treads were almost imperceptible in places. Bassam walked up easily. I had to clamber up on all fours. He lit a fire and started to make tea. I began to explore.

We were on a wide ledge whose area was greater than the wadi floor below. The ground fell away to the right and I followed it. I took two or three steps down against the rock face, saw an apparent man-made waterfall to my right, with a pool at its base, and realised that I was standing on the terrace of a once substantial, free-standing house. How my heart leapt in wonder that I should be standing in such a place, where centuries before, people had literally carved out an elegant, well-defended life for themselves.

Just then, from high up in the rocks, came a shout. Bassam answered. Some words were exchanged. I returned to the fire and asked what had been said. The shepherd had asked what we were doing. "Making tea," Bassam had told him. He was content but he stayed above, watching us. He was obviously the self-appointed guardian of this special place.

Then Bassam said,

"Go up these steps and turn left at the top."

"Which steps?" I asked. Bassam pointed to a cleft in the rock, against the cliff face. I went in the direction he had indicated and, having fought my way past some overhanging oleanders, I was able to see another flight of steps cut into the rock. In this sheltered place, these steps were less eroded, but the risers were quite deep and negotiating the flight in that heat, maybe 28 degrees, was quite exhausting. So, with my heart pounding from the effort, I took the left turn at the top and picked my way across a rock-strewn incline towards another cleft in the rocks. This one was only four feet wide. Carved in the rock was a niche with an arched top. It felt as if I were approaching a place of worship.

Indeed I was. The short cleft led me into a partially-excavated courtyard. On my left was a triclinium, a three-sided dining room. Next to it was a kitchen and adjacent to that a large water cistern cut into the solid rock. I climbed some steps to the right and there, before me was the most important room. It was larger than all the others and its back wall was covered with niches. The pillars which would have flanked its sides like a proscenium arch were now unceremoniously horizontal, victims of one of the many earthquakes which had changed the face of this land over millennia. Immediately in front of me was a vertical cross-section of the detritus which had built up on the floor of this chamber. It was three feet deep and had been carefully cut back by the archaeologists who had been working here. There were layers of small stones, layers of goat droppings, the charcoal from countless fires and small pieces of carved masonry.

I climbed onto the unexcavated section of floor and tried to interpret my surroundings. Unusually, the back wall had a window cut into it, allowing light to penetrate the depths of the chamber. My eyes followed the line of light and then I saw it. It was a stone beam above the window. Carved on the surface was a Greek inscription of four lines or so. The ancient energy of this place pervaded every pore of my body right through to my bone marrow. Here was a holy place. Here was a shrine which had attracted pilgrims for over two thousand years. What had been seen or felt here? Had someone seen a vision? Did the rocks have unusual powers? The dining-room, the kitchen, the cisterns and whatever still lay beneath the tumbled rocks were all there to meet the domestic needs of those who had come to worship here.

I re-visited this place many times over the years. It was a one and a half hour walk from the village. I would make tea on the kitchen floor and then fall asleep using a rock as a pillow. There was no doubt in my mind that, every time I left, I was taking a special, spiritual energy with me. Whatever had attracted those pilgrims was still there.

I descended from the excavation, feeling that I had been treading on holy ground. Bassam was not at the fire. I was pleased; grateful for the opportunity to think and to assimilate the experience. This land was special and I felt a very close connection to it. I began to think about re-shaping my retirement plans. I wanted to make a home here. After a while, Bassam returned and I tried to tell him all that was in my heart.

He explained that, because Petra is a world heritage site, the land there can be acquired only by people with tribal rights or by Government allocation, like the land for Um Sayhoun itself. Not even Jordanians from the north are permitted to make purchases here. However, he had an idea. Three years previously, he had bought some land in the village from his uncle. In addition, Fatma had recently received her share of her father's estate. He had owned some valuable land on the road to Taybah. It had been sold after his death and she and her ten siblings had each received four thousand dinars, approximately three and a half thousand pounds. Bassam told me with great pride that Fatma had recently said to him,

"You can have my money. Let us build a house on our land."

Bassam's idea was that I should contribute to the building costs and that he would create a small home for me within the new building. The family would occupy the whole of one floor and I would occupy half of the lower floor. Since the house was to be built into the steep wadi side, the view of the mountains would still be clear, even from the lower level.

I agreed to his proposal. We shook hands and that was that. No paperwork. No lawyers. My contribution was appropriate to the portion I would occupy. I never had cause to regret that handshake in Wadi Nameer. Bassam said,

"I will never forget what you are doing to help me." And he didn't. He told all his family, his tribe and the village about the arrangement. That was to be Joanna's home, forever.

Work on the house began in the Spring of 2006. On each weekend visit, there were exciting questions to be answered. Did I want a European or an Arab toilet? How much tiling did I want in the bathroom and kitchen? Where was the best place for my car?

At that time, it would have suited me financially to have taught for longer than the original two-year contract, and the possibility of doing so was certainly there. Late in the Autumn term, the management had asked the usual questions of availability for the following year. Something had made me stall in giving my response and time was running out.

During my Christmas break in the UK that year, I met a friend for coffee. He was full of a new contact he had made. This woman was amazing. She had put him in touch with his Overself. Well, I wasn't certain what that was but my heart gave the sort of lurch that I had learned was a call to action. So, I asked for her contact details and got in touch. She was about to spend five weeks in an Indian Ashram but would be flying back through Abu Dhabi in order to give a course on her stopover. I didn't want to do her course but we arranged that I would fly there from Amman and speak to her after her day's work was done.

She knew very little of me. We were both simply responding to impulses that we should meet. She held my hands, was silent for a minute, then said,

"You should get away from that school and spend more time with the Bedouin." That was enough for me. Call it a sign or not, it certainly helped to gel my thoughts. I told the school management that I planned to retire at the end of the academic year and, by the end of August, I was living in the Bedouin village.

Chapter 8
My New Home

By Um Sayhoun standards, my house was palatial. It had floor to ceiling tiles in the bathroom and kitchen and all the walls were plastered. In many of the homes, the inside walls were bare breeze-blocks. There was an entrance hall large enough for four or five neighbours and their children to sit and enjoy a tea break. The sitting room had dual aspect windows onto the mountains and the wadi below. I had ordered some *tagliss arabi,* or Arabic seating from a shop in Wadi Musa. This consisted of upholstered, thicker foam mattresses with separate backs and elbow rests. There was also a wall unit for the television. In most homes, this piece of furniture was the 'hearth' of the home. Multi-coloured plastic flowers would be woven into the wrought-iron frame. It was also the repository for all things valuable; the phone charger, medicines, school reports when they came in, and ash-trays.

The house had electricity and running water but, at first, no means of heating the water. I had to wait for six months before I had help in buying and installing a geyser. All the window frames were metal and each window was protected by an ornate, external wrought-iron grid. When talking to tourists, the Petra Bedouin would boast of the honesty of their neighbours. They could leave their doors open and no-one would enter the house, they said. If someone found a five-dinar note on the street, he would try to find the owner. Indeed, I was once asked to collect and forward the belongings of a lady from New Zealand. When I went to the place where she had lived, the neighbours showed me her things. They also said that a boy had found her purse in a big refuse bin and had taken it to Abu Shadi, a well respected local man. I went to his house. He knew of me and was happy to hand over the purse. It contained nearly 400 dinars [£350] in cash, a cash card and the key to her car. At Abu Shadi's suggestion, I left a 20 dinar reward for the boy who had recovered the purse. Nevertheless, every ground-floor window and most first floor windows too, were covered with a grid.

There were no cavity walls. There were circular fluorescent lights in each room. The lives of these bulbs and their motors were extremely limited. The intermittent flickering of a poor bulb was unbearable. I bought two standard lamps with dimmer switches which were a godsend. Bassam and his family simply plugged light bulbs directly into the thirteen amp wall sockets.

My water supply came from a tank on the flat roof. As drought became more of a problem, the local Government opened the taps to replenish our tanks only three times a week. Bassam and Fatma were using their water not only for the family, but also for their two mules, two donkeys and, when the trough - on the site where many families kept their goats overnight – ran dry, their fifteen goats. It took me a while to realise that, when their tank was empty, they used a piece of hose to siphon water from my tank into theirs. I had no warning when my tank was about to run dry. On more than one occasion, I had to have a strip-wash using bottled water. In later years, when the monthly water bills arrived, they stopped asking me for a contribution.

Some friends in Amman had given me, by way of a house-warming present, some fine mesh with appropriate adhesive to create bug screens at all the windows. One of the first jobs I did was to cut them up and stick them in the apertures. My neighbours had never seen anything like it but, interestingly, none of them wanted the leftover mesh despite the fact that our windows were wide open for ten months of the year. That mesh was wonderful against mosquitoes and tiny, delta-winged insects with a savage bite that the Bedouin called *ba'othas* or biters. I couldn't construct a bug screen for the door, so hung fine, cotton net curtains to try to keep the insects at bay. Unfortunately, visits from my neighbours often meant the arrival of illegal immigrants, carried in on their clothing.

The bedroom window opened onto the back of the house, directly against the vertical rock face, five feet away.

The writer's home.

This narrow strip formed a kind of open-ended tunnel running under the concrete terrace of the home above. It funnelled beautiful cool air in the heat of the day but was also a rat-run for escaping naughty boys.

The shower room and toilet were next. There was a window space high on the wall, but no glazing. Originally, this was the only window in the house which did not have security bars over it. That situation was quickly remedied. One weekend, after I had furnished the house but had not yet started to live in it, I discovered that someone, probably a boy, had climbed in. The dimensions of the window were 18" x 13". Apart from the dirty marks on the tiles below the window and the broken soap holder, which had been used as a step, there was clearer evidence that someone had been in the house. A washing-up bowl and a box had been brought through from the kitchen. Having gained entry to the house, the perpetrator had been unable to make his escape without some means of reaching the window whose lower edge was seven feet up.

Finally came the kitchen. This had a large porcelain sink, some storage units which quickly fell apart, a cooker fired by a gas cylinder and a fridge-freezer. I had ordered these items in Amman. They had been delivered from Aqaba. There had been no charge despite the delivery requiring the negotiation of the eighteen steep, uneven steps which led from the dirt track down to my front door.

My appearance in the village was an entertainment far superior to television. Giggling girls came to my door with lame excuses. Neighbours arrived to drink tea and inspect the house.

"Ah...*haylo*," they would say. "Lovely."

The Petra donkey men all spoke English, to a greater or lesser degree. Here in the village, among the women, it was Arabic. I had taken weekly lessons in standard Arabic from a colleague in Amman, but the Bedouin dialect was something else entirely. I learned later that the Arabic which they spoke, more closely resembled the language of the seventeenth century. The world, with its changing language, had entirely passed these people by.

Each evening, after a day of trying to understand and be understood, I was exhausted. My television signal provider was Nilesat. Its selection of programmes left a lot to be desired. Fortunately, I had amassed a library of DVDs and spent most evenings watching one of these. For the first two weeks, however, even this quiet time was interrupted. At about 9 o'clock each evening, there would be a tap at the door. It was Fatma who was visiting, apparently, for no particular reason. Tea was made and we struggled to converse for half an hour before she rose and left. Bassam was in the habit of returning from his work in Petra at mid to late afternoon. He would have his meal and shower and then would go out again until bedtime. He was either at his mother's house or at a gathering of the men. His mother had recently been widowed, Ali having died in the Spring. All were agreed that he was about a hundred years old. It seemed reasonable to me that, in these circumstances, Fatma would like some company.

It was towards the end of a fortnight, when I overheard Fatma talking to a friend on her balcony above and partially understood what was said, that I discovered the reason for the visits. She had been acting on Bassam's instructions. He wanted her to check that I was alone downstairs and not keeping company below his house. This realisation was such a disappointment to me. We had spent hours together in the mountains over two years. Had he made no assessment of the kind of life I was likely to lead in the village? It wasn't the first and it wouldn't be the last time in this society that the only possible explanation, motivation or reason for any given action was assumed to be either money or sex.

When we first lived in the house, there was no boundary wall. A popular cut across the wadi passed over Bassam's land. Its route was evident from the smoothly-worn path through the rocks. The passers-by, usually men, tried to be as unobtrusive as possible. Their eyes were always down until they were well past the house. Out in the mountains, when walking past a goats' hair tent, it was important to pass on the closed side. This situation was nevertheless unacceptable to Bassam and his family. A wall had to be built.

This was no mean feat, given that Bassam's land fell away quite steeply to the wadi bottom. One day a lorry appeared and delivered breeze-blocks and cement. A gang of Egyptian workers soon followed. They worked very efficiently and quickly produced an enclosure, eight courses high. One rectangle designated the boundary. The other, running at right angles from the boundary wall to the corner of my house, provided a private area for me on the side of the main building. It was very barren land, extremely rocky and dusty. It supported very little vegetation. The most common forms of flora or fauna were ants and cockroaches. They had colonised the wadi and we had invaded their territory.

In later years, Fatma decided to plant fruit trees around the wall of my 'garden'. It took two Egyptians and an enormous pick-axe to get them into the ground. There were a palm tree, two pomegranate trees, two lemon trees, an apricot tree and a grape vine. They were slow to establish themselves, partly because water was so scarce and expensive and partly because passing goats and donkeys waited for the new growth and then had a feast. In order to prevent this, Fatma was keen to add two or three more courses of breeze blocks to the wall, but Bassam argued against that because of the effect it would have on my view of the mountains. Gradually, aided by my used washing-up water, the trees thrived and eventually produced fruit, not always abundantly.

There are five major family groups in Um Sayhoun; one of the most influential is the Fagara (or Al Faqeer.) Many of their properties lay along the main road through the village, giving them easy access to passing tourists. In addition, they were well placed to build shops, cafes or camping equipment stores. The sheikh of the village is a member of this family. The other groups are the Mowassa, the Jedailet, the Jamada and the Samaheen. It is to the latter group that Bassam, his family and therefore I belonged. On our rides to *Al Barra* and our meetings with the old man, Salaama, Bassam always introduced me thus,

"Hi Joanna, hiya min Samaheen, this is Joanna, she is from the Samaheen."

Bassam and Fatma have five children; Chofa, Jasmine, Ahmad, Ayeesha and Abdullah. At the time that I started to live below them, their ages ranged from eleven to four years.

Bassam's old house had been in a neighbourhood dominated by the Samaheen family. The same was not true of his new house, although a line of uncles did occupy houses in the row above ours. The brothers are called Ghasm, Gassam and Gasseem. Their sisters, all married and living in other neighbourhoods, are Ghasma, Gassama and Gasseema. They are the half-siblings of H'layla, Bassam's mother. Gassam had married a Swiss lady and had settled in her country. He let his house and stayed with Gasseem when he came to visit.

Gasseem and his wife, Airlia, are among my favourite people. Like everyone else, they married young. Airlia had eight children by the time she was twenty eight; six boys and two girls. Their yard is tiled but, at the side, is a wonderful, mature apricot tree which faithfully bears fruit year after year. It also provides wonderful shade under which to while away the hottest hours of the day.

Airlia was from the Fagara family. I gradually became aware that Gasseem allowed Airlia extraordinary freedom. She and a female relative once spent a week at the home of other family members in Amman. A couple of years after that, she and her mother joined a coach party from the village which was going on the *hajj* pilgrimage to Mecca. While she was away, I, like other neighbours, called by with cooked food, fruit and vegetables for her family. On her return she gave me three lovely gifts from Saudi Arabia.

One day, not long after I started to live in the village, I was taking a narrow shortcut to the main road. It ran along the side of Gasseem's land. I could hear crying and excited children's voices. Two children, no more than toddlers, ran towards me and indicated that I should follow. They led me into Gasseem's yard and to the steps of his house. The elder of his two daughters, Soomaya, was sitting on the steps, crying, her face covered by her bloodied hands. She had fallen from a high wall and had cracked the bottom off one of her front teeth. She must have been about nine or ten at that time, so the tooth was an adult one. Neither of her parents was at home.

I knew no Arabic words to comfort her, so I sat beside her and stroked her back and her cheeks, quietly uttering English words of comfort. She raised her head, read the expression of compassion on my face and promptly climbed onto my lap for comfort. A calm fell on the assembled children. We sat like that for maybe three minutes and then Fatma arrived. She looked in the girl's mouth and there followed a conversation which was beyond my comprehension. I helped the child from my lap and left her in Fatma's care. I felt good. She had been comforted and she and I had established a connection that never dulled. She was the most beautiful child with the captivating eyes of a woman.

For several weeks, or even months, she smiled less, not wanting to reveal the damaged tooth. It was some time before Gasseem was able to save enough money to pay for the required dentistry. The smile returned and her beauty shone. I am sure that she will marry young.

Gasseem, has a mule but he does not earn his living by transporting tourists. No. Gasseem is a musician. He plays the rababa, a kind of bowed lute. How I loved to listen to his singing and playing, usually after the sun had gone down and people ventured into their yards, safe from the sun's fierce rays. Gasseem makes a good living from his music. Three times a week, there is a special tourist excursion from the neighbouring town of Wadi Musa entitled Petra By Night. The siq and the area in front of the Treasury, *Al Khazneh*, are illuminated by myriad candles embedded in sand in brown paper bags. The effect is absolutely magical. Having processed quietly in order to soak up the atmosphere, the tourists gather for refreshments in front of Petra's most famous monument and there to entertain them is my friend and neighbour, Gasseem.

Fifty yards up the side alley from our house was the home of Fatma's mother, Hamda. Given that Bassam's and Fatma's fathers were brothers, she is also Bassam's aunt-in-law. She was in her early sixties when I first started to live in the village and had been widowed for about two years. She has six married daughters and one, Aisha, aged fourteen, still at home. She also has four sons, all of marriageable age at that time and yet none of whom were then married. Her home is on a large, flat plot. Her sons gradually built their own homes above, and attached to the back of, her property, rising to three storeys in places.

She has a kitchen in the house but, like several other homes, she also has an outhouse where a large open fire can be lit. It is here that she makes *shrak* and heats the enormous pots for *mansaf* and *magloba*. With four sons at home and frequent visits from her married daughters and their children, each meal needs to be a feast.

An accident in girlhood has left her without the index finger of her right hand. There is not even the vestige of a stump. The injury is barely noticeable. Only when you shake hands in greeting can you realise that there is less to grip. Hamda has a lovely, kind face, but sometimes it is clouded by pain. Like many of the women who have had multiple pregnancies, her knees are worn out and are very painful. She walks with a pronounced limp as she makes her daily trips to her goats and chickens on the other side of the main road.

She is well loved by her sons, her daughters and their husbands and her twenty seven grandchildren. She is a true matriarch.

It would be true to say that Bassam's family, particularly Fatma and her children, visited the homes of fellow Samaheen families more often than those of other family groups. One of Fatma's sisters had married into the Fagara and another into the Jedailet. Bassam was on very good terms with these brothers-in-law. He was also on reasonable terms with the men from the Fagara family who were our immediate neighbours. The same could not be said of Fatma and their wives.

Not long after we started living in the house, one of the neighbour's daughters, a particularly insolent child of about seven, climbed onto the dividing wall and started throwing stones at the tethered animals. Fatma went out to remonstrate with the child, who simply laughed, totally ignoring Fatma's requests to stop. I heard the commotion and went outside to add my support. I thought that Fatma was making a mistake in not moving towards the child, so I set off down the steep rocky slope, heading for the child. She began by treating me with similar contempt until she realised that I was prepared to walk right up to her and, if necessary, to pull her down from the wall.

At that point, she started crying loudly, jumped down onto her side of the wall and ran to her mother who, although aware of her daughter's bad behaviour, had chosen to ignore what was going on. A great performance then began. The neighbour came up to the wall brandishing a heavy stick, about two feet long. She and Fatma exchanged unintelligible insults, alternating facial expressions of menace and laughing contempt. I simply stood, for what it was worth, by Fatma's side. Other neighbours and their children watched through their windows or over garden walls. Eventually, while still hurling insults, the two women began moving apart and reversing towards their doors. The shouts turned to grumbling and then to mumbling as each disappeared into her home, both honours still intact. Always, thereafter, the naughty girl gave me a wide berth.

Other neighbours included Fatma (Um Hatim), Fatma's sister Hadeeja, another sister H'layla, two of Saloom's daughters [Saloom is one of the two lovely old ladies I met at the first wedding], Rami (the son of Marguerite van Geldermalsen author of Married to a Bedouin, Virago UK), Hamda's brother Awath (whose daughter had helped me protect Faisal in Chapter 1), Mahmoud (brother of Bassam Ali Salaama) and many others. Some of their stories will emerge as my tale unfolds.

This, then, was my new home and these were some of my neighbours. Over the years our lives were to become intermingled in many different ways. In the course of my life, I have battled cancer, injustice, unhappy marriages and physical pain, but nothing was to make me dig as deep into my reserves as the life that lay ahead of me in Um Sayhoun.

Chapter 9
Baptism of Fire

Noise. That was the instant and most constant trial. The summer lasted until December that year, with temperatures as high as the low 30s. The windows and door had to be left open to catch any breeze. My neighbour's television, whose volume must have been deafening to those in the same room, was on all day, whether or not there was anyone in the house. The man on the other side of the wadi, on his return home, played the car radio at such a pitch that I had to adjust the volume on my television in order to hear the broadcast. The frequent rows, usually between Bassam's two oldest daughters, sounded so blood-curdling that I occasionally went upstairs to intervene. At other times, if Chofa were getting the better of her younger sister, Jasmine would cry out,

"*Joanna ta'alee,* Joanna come!" Joanna was my name in the village. It was difficult for my neighbours to distinguish the difference in vowel sounds in the names John, Jean, June, Jane and Joan. So, by reverting to the nickname my brothers used, the problem was solved. What was actually said was "J'anna" with no attempt to sound the first vowel.

The calls to prayer five times a day, which were broadcast on the public address system on the mosque, were not in themselves unpleasant. However, on Fridays, the PA system was left on for the whole of the mid-morning prayer. This included the sermon. My Arabic was not good enough to understand what was being said and, indeed, even if that had not been the case, there would have been some difficulty because the volume was so high that the amplified sound was distorted. I didn't need to understand in order to have some impression of what was being said. The tone always seemed so angry and ranting. When Arab men meet on the street, be they the greatest of friends, the tone of their exchange is always so forceful and the delivery of their words so explosive, that the English ear is certain an argument is taking place. Such was the sound of the sermon. The only difference was that the aggressive tone and volume were maintained unabated for fully twenty minutes.

At night the animals took over the village. Every night and all night, at frequent intervals, the chorus was the same. Packs of dogs ran through the streets, every one of them barking as they went. Almost every man owned at least one donkey. Some owned camels too. These were kept at their homes, along with the chickens and cockerels, close to the locked grain stores. When the dogs were temporarily silent, the donkeys started. It was almost as if they were saying to each other,

"Did you hear that?"

"Yes. What a racket! You don't catch *us* disturbing everyone like that."

Only they said it several times, with increasing intensity. Bassam told a lovely story of a time when several families had taken themselves into the mountains for the night, preferring to sleep outdoors away from the village. On hearing a call to prayer, if the faithful cannot go immediately to the mosque, a form of words is uttered in acknowledgement of the call. This particular night, one of the men, thinking he had just heard the 4am call to prayer, lifted his head and spoke the words aloud. Everyone laughed. What he had just heard in his sleepy state was, in fact, a donkey.

In addition to the backdrop of sounds, there were two smells which were difficult to live with. Occasionally a man would set fire to a pile of goats' droppings. The smoke from these fires would drift among the houses all day, creeping into every room. It was a cloying, unpleasant smell. It was, at least, a natural product. The other smell was quite different. I was awoken one morning at about 6am by a throbbing sound. It seemed to go away and then return. The second time I heard it, it was accompanied by an acrid smell. At first I simply lifted the single sheet that was covering me and pulled it up over my nose. When both sound and smell persisted, I arose to investigate. A light pick-up was weaving in and out of the narrow lanes

Early-morning insecticide.

belching out white smoke from a machine with a 4 inch diameter exhaust which was mounted on the back. I, at least, always slept indoors. Most of my neighbours and their families slept outside or up on their roofs. There was no escape. I learned later that this was part of a government pesticide programme; an attempt to control the mosquitoes and other parasites. When the men became aware that the decontamination van was in the neighbourhood, they hurried to lead their animals, which were usually tethered to their garden walls, under cover. I am not sure whether the process had any effect but it was a terrible intrusion in our lives.

In the first chapter, I asked questions concerning the display of cruelty to the boy Faisal and about what sort of society could produce such cruelty. I hadn't been living long in the village before I saw that there was nothing unusual in this. I was also given a savage insight into its roots, in the relationship that most of men and boys had with their animals.

I was sitting quietly in my house one afternoon, sheltering from the burning sun. I had become used to, if not inured to, a favourite pastime of the local boys. They would tie string or electricity cable around the necks of two dogs and goad them into fighting each other. The barking of the dogs was a terrible sound. In my judgement, the sounds they made were not a challenging prelude to the fight but cries of desperation. How can we best survive this? Shall we pretend to fight until they get bored and find something else to do? Alerted to such an incident shortly after my arrival, I had shouted across the wadi where a group of boys had gathered. They simply laughed at me and ran away out of my sight. No other adult intervened.

The sound this particular afternoon was so desperate and so close to my house that I went outside and followed the noise. I went up the steps and along to the gap between Bassam's house and our immediate neighbours. The neighbour's teenage son, surrounded by about six younger children, was holding a ten week old puppy in his hands. I was spared the sight of what had caused the creature to cry out because the youngsters shouted at him,

"*J'anna ta'al. J'anna ta'al.* Joanna's coming. Joanna's coming."

"*Inta cowie?* Does that make you feel brave?" I asked. The children could see how angry I was and they ran to their homes. The boy slunk away, laughing as he went. I returned to my house, hoping that the incident was over. It wasn't. The punishment for my audacity was swift in coming. Less than twenty minutes later, Bassam's daughter Jasmine came to my door. I didn't understand what she said, so she led me outside. She turned into the covered area that lay between the back of my house and the wadi wall. At the far end, a heavy metal grill had been put across the tunnel, to prevent the neighbours' children from running under the house and looking through my back windows. Hanging on the grill by one of his back paws was the puppy. There was no sound from him. I approached, fearing that he was dead. He was alive, his heart beating so fiercely that it nearly burst out of his little body. He was too traumatised to make a sound. I tried to reassure him as I took the weight of his body in my hands. His paw was bleeding from the thin wire which had been used to suspend him. Jasmine took him from me so that I could release the wire from the grill. He submitted meekly as we took him to my house, removed the wire from his paw and bathed the wound. Jasmine explained that the puppy belonged to the father of the perpetrator. I went to the house but no one answered. I hid the creature under some scattered timber, hoping that he could hide there until the father was in the house. Jasmine told her father that night. It was not considered sufficiently important for Bassam to mention it to his neighbour.

About three months later, we were blessed by the arrival of some heavy rainfall, accompanied by thunder and lightning. There simply isn't enough rainfall in the south of Jordan, and there hasn't been for several years. The women take the goats into the mountains but there is no grass. *Burseem,* a kind of dried alfafa has to be bought to supplement the animals' diet. I was in Wadi Musa when the skies opened and had to drive home very carefully on the winding, newly wet, mountain road.

On my return home, I found rainwater running down the inside wall under the window in my lounge. The driving rain had found its way around the poorly-fitting metal window frames and had soaked the seating along that wall. I put towels in place and tried to stop the water escaping further into the room. It was mid-afternoon and I had to put the lights on because it was so dark. At one particularly loud clap of thunder, the lights went out as the electricity failed.

I needed to return to my car to collect the shopping. As I went up the steps, it was still raining. Two of another neighbours' daughters ran to the car when they saw me approaching. They pointed to their brother, a boy of about four. He was a bit further off, standing over something on the ground, throwing stones. I wasn't sure what he was doing but I shouted through the pouring rain,

"*Hallas. Hathee mush kwiez.* Stop that. It is not good." He looked up, stopped and seemed to move away but, by the time I had returned to my car and opened the boot, he had found three more stones and had started again. I ran through the rain to where he was. A tiny, sodden puppy of about eight weeks was cowering against a stone which was about half its size. This four-year-old was throwing stones at it from point blank range. As I approached him, he stopped what he was doing but only to offer me his right hand, to shake in greeting. I ignored it, grabbed him by the scruff off the neck and frog-marched him towards his home, saying "Go to your home." He started to cry: not because he was afraid of getting into trouble, but because I had not been friendly and had put a halt to his game. I am quite certain that he had no idea that what he was doing was wrong. Many of the Bedouin keep dogs. Their chief purpose is to guard the sheep and goats at night. Wolves are a real and constant threat in the mountains. So, dogs have a value but they are also utterly despised. Could part of the answer for the stoning of the disabled boy lie in this? Recent research has demonstrated that those who are cruel to animals are more likely to mistreat their fellow man. I wonder.....

That first winter was by far the coldest of the eight that I spent in the village. The house walls were almost useless. The difference in temperature between the inside and outside was negligible. At night the temperatures dipped to near freezing. I retreated to the lounge. I ate there, slept there, watched the television news there and did my ablutions there. Without a geyser, I had to boil the kettle for hot water. I used a dedicated plastic washing-up bowl for strip washes in front of the calor gas stove. Once the sun rose, it was always warm enough to heat the air, whatever the time of year. It didn't reach my doorstep until noon. I could then shift my centre of activity to the hall, or to the rough, compacted earth of the back yard.

Spring came and, with it, the cockroaches and ants. They had colonised that side of the wadi long before our house had been built there. One morning I awoke to find eight cockroaches on the route from my bed to the bathroom and a further six in the shower tray. I quickly bought a powerful aerosol whose effectiveness was claimed to last for three months. I would say that that was a justifiable claim. The only difference was that the cockroaches that I now found were all on their backs, dead. Three years later, I had earthenware tiles laid in the yard. That made a big difference, but it didn't stop me from laying down the precautionary three-month spray.

The ants were more of a problem. In the long summers, the battle against them was constant. It led me to be extremely disciplined as to food management and storage. I used a cool box as a dry-goods store. I once put some leftover cake in there. Never again. By the time that I noticed, the column of ants stretched from a crack behind the cooker, down the wall, along the work surface, down the cupboard, over the floor, across the tiles, up the side of the cool box and through the seal which I had foolishly judged tight enough.

Despite their nuisance indoors, I learned to admire the ants. I spent many hours, sitting on the step, watching them operate. A single ant could haul a grain of wheat three times its size. Occasionally, knowing the effort that was required, a second ant would join in. It was a magnificent example of co-operation; one pulling and the other pushing. As they approached the entrance to the nest, other ants gave way to them allowing enough room to drag the prize into the nest entrance.

Summer came and all my neighbours began to sleep outside. It was a pre-retiring performance of some complexity for Fatma to set up the mattresses and mosquito netting each night. She also had two two-man tents and some of the children slept in them. Lovely as I am sure it would have been, to have slept under the stars, I never did. My reaction to any bite was very uncomfortable; the effects often lasting, despite effective creams, for three to four days. No, I thought, I am better off indoors.

For most of that first June, the nights were not unpleasantly hot. I was still in the habit, however, of setting the timer on my room fan. One night, I set it for forty minutes – long enough to allow me to read in comfort and to switch the light off and settle - and went to bed. My bed at that time was two foam mattresses on the floor, held together by an under blanket and a fitted sheet. I had a top sheet and, that night, I had added a light duvet cover. The electric fumakiller for mosquitoes and other flying biters was plugged in, giving the room a red glow. The windows, covered with their bug screens, were all open. I read for a while, pushed my wax earplugs into position, and turned off the light. The room was pleasantly cool, thanks to the fan, and sleep came quickly.

At some point in the night, something caused me to start lifting out of my sleepy state. I was on my back with my arms resting on the top cover. I could feel something on the inside of my left arm. In my sleepiness I lifted my right arm to investigate what was happening on my left arm. No sooner had it come into contact with whatever was there, than a searing pain hit the palm of my right hand. I threw off the covers, rose and immediately took out the ear plugs. I needed to know what and where the thing was and didn't want to miss any signal that might give me its position.

I put the light on and plastered some anti-histamine cream onto my palm. All this was within a minute and already my fingers were almost numb and I could feel the poison moving up to my wrist. I had already decided that I must go upstairs to the family: first, because I was afraid of losing consciousness whilst alone and, second, because they would know whether I needed to go to hospital. However, before I could go up to them, I needed to identify what had caused the pain. It was 02.10.

I fetched a powerful anti-cockroach aerosol from the kitchen and began very gingerly to lift off the covers. The removal of the top duvet cover revealed nothing. I had just begun to lift the top sheet when a cream flash raced for the bottom pillow. It was then that I first suspected that the culprit was a scorpion. I removed the top pillow and sprayed the edge of the lower pillow. I pulled it away but there was nothing there. I thought it had made it to the top edge of the mattresses, so I pulled them away from the wall. Still nothing. I then turned the pillow over and there it was. It took 4-5 long blasts of the spray before it stopped trying to move. I brought a small glass from the kitchen and used a piece of card to trap the scorpion inside. It was about an inch and a quarter long. It was hard to believe that it had packed such a punch.

I put my dressing gown on and wound up my torch. Clutching that and the glass I opened the door and went out into the night. I had to climb the twelve external steps to my neighbours' house. The whole family was asleep on their balcony. I knew that Bassam was a lighter sleeper than Fatma because they had told me. However, it would have been unthinkable for me to be calling out a man's name in the middle of the night. So, I stayed outside the low wall surrounding their property, as close to them as I could get and started to call "Fatma. Fatma." No answer. I repeated the calls. Still no answer. Then two donkeys nearby started braying. There was no point in repeating myself in the face of such a racket. All this time I was monitoring my body to try to assess how much of an emergency this was. The pain in my hand was almost unbearable.

Eventually the donkeys ceased and I tried again. This time I was rewarded by a sleepy voice saying "*Meen*?

Who?" I didn't know the Arabic for scorpion so I said that a bad small animal had bitten me. The mosquito net was lifted and Fatma appeared in her nightgown. I showed her the body and she said,

"*Agrab, larkin sareer, al hamdu lillah*. It is a scorpion but small. Thank God." Bassam, who had probably nudged Fatma awake, called from under the mosquito net, wondering at the cause of the disturbance.

Fatma took me into her house and fetched sugar and two slices of potato from her kitchen. The greatest pain was on the palm of my right hand, but there was also pain on my left forearm. She explained that this mixture would draw the poison out. We sat for an hour pressing to potato to my skin. I felt the poison creep half way up my right forearm but no further. I asked whether I should go to hospital. She thought not, because the scorpion was a juvenile.

After an hour I said that I was happy to return to my house. So, with thanks and apologies for disturbing her sleep I went. I washed the sticky mixture off my arms and changed the bed linen which had been drenched by the insecticide. I felt strangely calm and ready to sleep again.

The following morning, my story was the talk of the neighbourhood. The cream scorpions are the most feared because the bite of the adult can be lethal if not treated quickly. Bassam had always taught me to lift stones carefully when making a fire, and to check underneath. We had done that on one of our mountain rides and had uncovered a fully-grown cream scorpion hibernating. Bassam took a sharp stick, pierced its 'heart' and threw it over the cliff. So, a procession of neighbours visited me.

" *Al Hamdu lillah as salaamah*. Thank God you came back." These same words are used to a woman who has been safely delivered of a child.

So, my baptism of fire had consisted of noise, smells, animal cruelty, punishment for caring, cold, cockroaches and a scorpion. Why didn't I pack up and leave? How had I borne it all? I can only say that, every time I needed it, I found the strength to cope; not only strength. I felt an amazing calm. I had felt anger but I never panicked and, what is more, I never felt fear. I had followed my heart and a love of the mountains in coming to settle in Um Sayhoun. I was now beginning to wonder whether I was there for some other purpose. Might it be that, by just quietly living here among the people, I could show, in some small way, a different model of behaviour?

Chapter 10

Three Weeks in Winter

On my visits to England, many people asked me, "But what do you DO all day in Jordan? I tried to give honest replies but could only manage the headlines. My friends, however, were not satisfied with the headlines. So, for three weeks in February 2008, I kept a journal. The effort of doing so was enormous. Each day was filled with the unexpected. Each day brought new challenges and demanded more and more of the energy which I had to give. By the evening, when the entries were written, I was numb with tiredness.

2008

8th February I finally picked up my car from Wadi Seer (Amman), with a new radiator and head gasket. I also took advantage of being in Amman to buy supplies which are unavailable in the south; rice pasta, butternut squashes, All Bran and the like. The journey back was smooth. On my return, Bassam's children appeared from nowhere to help carry my bags, always hopeful that I had brought some treats for them. [Usually, I had.] Cleaned the lounge – my living *and* sleeping quarters during the winter. I bring one of the bedroom mattresses through and put it on a seating mattress [because it has more 'give' in it.] I have lots of bedclothes and I wear my black sheepskin hat!! I must look a fright but I am warm and I sleep well. In the morning I can just put my hand out of bed and switch on the Halogen electric heater, so that it can take the chill off the air before I get up.

The phone has been cut off even though no bills have been sent. I was invited upstairs for supper.

9th February Phone shop closed. I decided to give myself a day off. I took the mountain road and spent the day in Wadi Araba (a thousand metres lower than us and warm.) Wonderful. In the evening, I took H'layla into Wadi Musa to have a photo taken for new, widow's ID.

10th February I hand-washed my dirty linen then, before setting off for Wadi Musa, I called on H'layla for the money for the new photos. I waited for 35 minutes outside the Phone shop 10.55-1130 but it still didn't open. I gave up and went to the Post Office to renew my PO box subscription. On my return to the village, I drank tea with Fatma, then went home to write a letter to my mother.

Mid-afternoon I returned to Wadi Musa to try to get my broadband reconnected but the Orange shop was still closed. I spent two hours at the Crowne Plaza catching up on my emails, using their wi-fi. I ate supper with Sa'ood's family.

11th February. Housework. 9.30 Aisha [Fatma's 13 year old sister] called. She wanted scissors to cut the bottom off her jeans. [The women are fully clothed under their *fustans*] She stayed for tea and xmas cake, then helped me hang out the washing on the airer. She wants to visit her grandfather (Salaama of *Al Barra*) in hospital this afternoon. A week Friday she wants me to take her and two other girls to a teacher in Wadi Musa for extra tuition. Aisha stayed an hour. Within 10 minutes of her going Fatma and Chofa came. They had been to the dentist in Wadi Musa for Chofa to have a filling. They had heard from Aisha that there was tea and xmas cake downstairs. I was making tea for them when the gas cylinder ran out, so the pot was carried upstairs to be finished off.

I made another visit to Wadi Musa in the hope of finding the phone shop open. I called at Fatma's sister So'mah on the way. I knew that her sister Tamam was there with her new baby, for whom I had a small gift [J10.] My first call in Wadi Musa was at the vegetable market, the *souq al hudra*. The phone shop was still closed. No notice on the door. Nothing.

On the way back, I made the mistake of thinking I would have lentil soup for lunch at the hotel. The lentil soup "wasn't available" but they had *fareeka* [a grain, a bit like pearl barley.] It had to be cooked from fresh and would take half hour. Over an hour later it arrived and was, indeed, delicious. Home to rest in the sun in my hallway.

Aisha called again repeating her request to go to the hospital to see her grandfather. It was decided that a group would go tonight. I was invited to Fatma's for supper. Hadeeja, Hamda and two of her sons were also there. There was much discussion both before and after supper about who should go. Eventually, too many of the family tried to get into my car. They were shouting at each other and pushing and shoving. So I got out and said "Tell me when you are ready." The result was that Fatma returned home. H'layla was in the front with So'mah, Hadeeja and Aisha in the back. Off we went.

A male cousin was already there. The old man was in good form. His lower leg was very swollen. The skin was very shiny with the pressure. I reminded him that I had met him three times before on *Al Barra*. Most of Hamda's daughters are overweight but Salaama singled out So'mah and asked her very discreetly, if she were pregnant. We stayed half an hour or so, then stopped at the desserts shop in Wadi Musa for Hadeeja and H'layla to buy cakes for their children.

12th February. I rose early to be in time for the calor gas delivery. It arrived at 7.45. The price of gas bottles has doubled to six and half JD. I did some housework. Some things just have to be done daily; wiping away layers of dust and sand, collecting the remains of cockroaches exposed to the lethal insecticide I spray in the cracks and checking that the ants are being kept at bay.

I received a call from a friend in Amman, asking for help with a hotel booking this weekend for a party of six people. I still can't make external calls or connect to the internet.

I went to Wadi Musa for coffee and to read the daily paper at the Crowne Plaza. I checked my emails while I was there. The hotel is full this weekend because of Valentines' Day. I then went to Petra Palace, the hotel preferred by the group from Amman, and made their bookings at a good rate.

The Orange shop was closed again. Later, on returning to my car, I noticed that it had opened. Knowing that my Arabic wasn't yet good enough to explain my problem, I rang my friend Amjad, who runs the souvenir shop in the Crowne Plaza. Less than five minutes later, he arrived with his young son, Omar. He really is a lovely man. Most men are happy to greet me and talk if I meet them at the hotel. It is a different story, however, if I meet them on the street in the face of their neighbours. Amjad is different. He shows no fear or unease and is always ready to help me.

It emerged that my landline problem was two-fold. The first was that all numbers starting with 0, that is, all but local numbers, are not available to foreigners to dial unless they pay JD 150 a year. Without that, only phone cards can be used. We went to the computer shop and I then realised that I had omitted some digits from the dial-up number. So, the second problem was of my own making. I returned home, tried using the card and succeeded at last at getting back online. Hurray!

Chofa and Jasmine came down to my door, hoping for some lunch. Their mother, Fatma, was out in the mountains with her goats. [Goat herding is a wonderful source of freedom for the women of the village. Goats are valuable and their feed is expensive. Time spent in finding even meagre grazing in this parched land is time well spent. After caring for her family and keeping the house clean, tending the goats is the next most acceptable activity for a woman.] I told them to return after twenty minutes when the lentil soup would be finished. When it was ready, we sat in the sun on my front doorstep and ate our lunch. Chofa returned later with Ayeesha, the third sister and I gave her some soup too. An hour later I was trying to rest when Jasmine returned with Ayeesha. I made them weak coffee and offered xmas cake, hoping that it didn't contain any alcohol.

I was invited to supper at Tamam and Ali's, as a way of thanking me for my gift to the new baby. They have five lovely children, all under 6 yrs! I was on taxi duty again later, to take another group to visit Salaama at the hospital. This time my passengers were Fatma, So'mah, Chofa and Samur, So'mah's teenage daughter. I returned home at 8.15. exhausted.

13th February. I lay in bed for warmth and watched the BBC World News. After breakfast I spent an hour online emailing and doing the Times crossword. The sky looked heavy but I decided to go for a walk in *Wadi Aglad*, a beautiful enclosed, hidden *wadi* behind Little Petra. I packed my bag with my old metal tea-pot, blackened by many fires, sugar, tea-bags, a section of cinnamon stick, some bottled water and a cigarette lighter and set off. I needed to drive for ten minutes, first, and to park my car near the stalls that welcomed tourists to Little Petra. The stall-holders knew me and greeted me.

The sky cleared a little so there was intermittent warm sunshine. I wrapped up warm though because the *Siq Al Barid*, the very narrow entrance to the *wadi,* doesn't get the sun. I had used my green hessian bag with the long handles. I wasn't happy with the way I was carrying it on my shoulder. I needed both hands free to climb up the rocks out of the *siq*. Two thousand years ago, a staircase had been hewn out of the rocks but erosion and earthquakes had all but closed the gap with falling rocks. So, I took my bag off my shoulder and did what I had seen my neighbours do. I put the straps across my forehead and let the bag fall down my back. To my surprise I was able to do it immediately and it felt very comfortable. It was good to have both hands free.

Once into the *wadi,* I looked for a place to light a fire and make tea. I chose a flattened ledge to the left, just before the place where the head of the *wadi* narrows – a place where no passing "traffic" would see me. The luxury of uninterrupted time on my own, to sit and think was such a rarity back in the village that, on my days out, knowing that I would be a source of interest, I tried to stay hidden. [I became very good at it.]There was plenty of wood and I managed to start the fire at my first attempt. This was pleasing since the wood in shady places in winter can be a bit damp. I made tea and ate a piece of cake. I then built up the fire for warmth because I was in shadow and the temperature was relatively low.

The *Amareen* were as welcoming on my return as they had been on my arrival. They are the tribe whose ancestral lands include Little Petra. [Sections of the *siq* entrance to the *wadi* are quite wide and form an excellent natural amphitheatre with an amazing acoustic. It is a favourite venue for celebrities from Amman who want to entertain guests or to let their hair down. The *Amareen,* armed with their guns, patrol the surrounding rocks during these gigs, in order to ensure the complete safety of their visitors.]As I left, one woman, having failed to get me to drink tea, tried to sell me a coin but her husband quietened her as I explained that I had no money, only the sugar and tea that I had needed for my drink.

On my return home, I washed my hair because the sun had moved round onto my door and it was warm in the hall. In winter, it is a good, discreet, place for hair drying. Jasmine arrived and watched the whole process; me, bending over the kitchen sink, using a plastic beaker to bail the water from the sink to my head, the repetition as I tried to rinse out the soap and the performance of trying to comb the knots out of my long hair.

I then warmed some of yesterday's soup. Ayeesha, Jasmine's younger sister, had joined us by this time. Fortunately, there was enough left for three. H'layla, Fatma's sister, was upstairs asking about me. The girls explained that I was staying where I was – in my porch – because my hair was wet and flowing freely. It was important that I stayed in the privacy of my house. So, H'layla came down to see me and sat for a while. I offered soup but she wanted to get back to the baby who was asleep at home, supervised by the other children. With my visitors gone and my hair largely dry, I lay on a mattress in the sun in the hall and tried to rest. I was just drifting off when Jasmine returned. "Did I have any shampoo?"

"You know I have. You watched me wash my hair," I replied with some irritation. Pause. "Go on then, take it." She went through to the kitchen and returned, holding up the bottle.

"Is this it?" she said. I couldn't keep the irritation out of my voice.

"You watched me use it. What did you see? Take it and go." She looked very shamefaced and went.

When I awoke, I saw that she had been back and had placed what was left of the shampoo on the step. I drank coffee, ate cake, did the crossword and felt refreshed. I was invited to supper with the family upstairs tonight. Fatma had prepared *malfoof* –stuffed cabbage and vine leaves. The rest of the evening was quiet. Sally, a friend in Amman, called. We chatted for 20-30 minutes. She thinks I'm paying too much for the phone. I will investigate. Throughout our conversation, I was out in the cold hall. I must buy a telephone cable extension.

14th February, Valentine's Day – of which much is made here. I awoke at 8am, removed my ear plugs, switched on the electric fire without moving from my bed and watched the BBC World news. I ate breakfast and then had a strip wash in front of fire in lounge/sleeping room, using a washing-up bowl dedicated to that purpose. I was only just decent when Aisha came – for no apparent reason – and brought 5 eggs from their chickens. She watched as I put make-up on my face and watched as I put the black-clothes-wash to soak in the kitchen sink. She continued to watch as I checked and wrote emails. Then Fatma and Jasmine arrived. They had been seeing to the goats. The animals were not in the mountains today but were being kept on the edge of the village where the herds are penned at night. They stayed and drank tea and ate rice cakes with peanut butter.

Ten minutes after they had left, while I was washing the soaked clothes Ali, Thraya's 11 year old son, arrived from school wearing just a thin sweater and coughing. He was cold, hungry and thirsty. He too had rice cake and peanut butter. This is alien food for these villagers but they seemed to enjoy it. I gave him a warm sweater from a bag of clothes that friends in Amman had given me to use as I saw fit. When the soup was ready he had some of that too. I told him that I needed to go to Wadi Musa and I put on my outdoor clothes.

My timing was perfect. No sooner had I dressed for departure than two of Ali's sisters and five of their friends arrived, also from school, hoping for fruit juice and something to eat. I was able to say that I was going out and they could see that it was the truth.

I went first to the chemist because Fatma wanted some sun block for when she is out with her goats. She had given me JD 4 but I could only see creams costing JD 12 and 13. The man was very nice and found a factor 40 costing JD 6 so I bought that, and some dental floss for myself. I then went to the Crowne Plaza for coffee and biscuits and read the Jordan Times. I was interrupted by Omar, the Training Manager, who doesn't seem to have enough to do.

On the way back home the *shergiya*, the south wind, was blowing very hard and I could see that it was raining heavily further up the mountain. A woman, her son, daughter and puppy were struggling against the wind as they walked on the roadside. I stopped. She and her daughter accepted a lift.

I ate some soup for lunch and started to write this journal. Fatma arrived. I explained about the sun block. She was pleased and gave me the extra JD 2. I offered her some soup which she accepted. She invited upstairs for supper tonight. She needed some garlic so I told her to help herself from the fridge. The Amman friend called and I gave him the directions to the Petra Palace Hotel. His party is travelling down tonight.

The weather is a cold 10 degrees and cloudy. I wrapped myself in a blanket and started to watch my DVD of *Atonement*. Jasmine 11yrs, came down and I told her it wasn't a suitable film for her to watch. She said she wanted to anyway. I said that what she wanted wasn't important. She left. She returned later briefly with Ayeesha because her mother needed a lemon. The film was nearly finished when I was called up to supper. The Amman friend called again while I was upstairs. Bad weather and poor visibility had caused them to make slow time. They had erroneously turned onto a minor road after Showbak so I explained the alternative route.

I returned home after supper and finished watching Atonement. It is Ian McEwan at his best – a dark side but redeemable. I then phoned the Amman party to see how they were getting on. They had reached Wadi Musa so I talked them down to their hotel. Aisha called and wanted me to change some Euros into dinars. I told her to come back tomorrow. I continued my reading of the Iliad then made my winter "camp" around the mattress in the lounge.

15th February. This being the Sabbath, went down to the Crowne Plaza for my weekly treat of breakfast out. There was intermittent sun so, on my return, I put yesterday's washing out on the drier. I decided to make some Welsh cakes in case the Amman party call in later. Fatma called in and wanted to borrow my vacuum cleaner. I explained that I needed to empty it first. She was interested in what the collection of dust looked like. Bassam called, wondering if I was at Petra with the Amman friends. I said that they hadn't telephoned but I gave him a description of them so that he could offer help if he saw them. Aisha came again. Her euro cents are worth half dinar but I didn't have any change. She wanted me to go to her house at 1pm and do some Reiki on her knees "As you did for my mother."

At 12.55 I went to Hamda's house to suggest that Aisha comes to my house for Reiki in order to have greater privacy. She was in the outhouse with her hands covered with flour, making *shrak*. She said she would come after 10 minutes. So I returned home and prepared the room. I waited, had some soup, waited, went to sleep in the sun in my hallway and she eventually came at 2.30pm. The session went well. She was relaxed and was, indeed, snoring by the time I had finished. I suggested she return on Monday.

Ken, the leader of the Amman expedition, called at 1.30pm to say that they had gone as far at the theatre and were back at their hotel! He invited me to dine with them and I suggested the Crowne Plaza. I then phoned Bassam and told him to stop looking out for Ken and his group. I went down to the Crowne Plaza for afternoon coffee and in order to book the table for tonight in person. Mahmoud, the lovely man who used to phone me on Thursday evenings to check that all was well on my journey from Amman at the weekends, was on duty on reception. I also saw Amjad at his shop in the hotel and thanked him for his help at the telephone shop. He too thinks that I am paying too much for the telephone line and has written a note for me in Arabic asking for an itemised bill. On my return, I sat in the last of the sunlight and darned the toes of my socks and tights. Fatma, Jasmine and Ayeesha arrived. I made tea with sage and offered Welsh cakes. When the sun went down I went back into the house and lit the calor gas fire.

Dinner At the Crowne Plaza was a great success. The staff were all so welcoming and attentive. Ali and Sarah's 5 year old daughter asked if I owned the hotel. I invited the group to coffee at my house tomorrow, before they drive on to Wadi Rum.

16th February. Ken called 40 minutes earlier than expected to say they were ready for the visit. I went up onto the village main street in order to guide them in up alley ways and through groups of children. They enjoyed the welsh cakes I had made. Ali wants to make a return visit and has my email and phone number. He wants to go to Jebel Haroun and maybe spend the night there. I said it could be done. Towards the end of their visit Aisha arrived. She sat in silence, waited till they had gone and then pronounced them "good people." She had brought a chocolate bar for me and said that her knees were very much better. Thank God.

She watched as I washed the dishes and, fortunately, went when she saw me get the computer out to sort my email. When that was done I went up to visit H'layla, Bassam's mother. I sat in the sun and she made tea. She said that her right heel was hurting and asked me to do Reiki after we had finished our tea. Fortunately it remained quiet with no grandchildren calling. After that we ate *bazeen*, a kind of home-made pasta, and talked. I asked her how she had felt as a 15 yr old girl, being married to Ali, more than 40 yrs her senior. She said that she had been very frightened but that he was a good man. We spoke a bit about her dead son, Abdullah. She doesn't like to look at photos of him. In fact, she won't. She said that her daughter

R'Kheeya needed Reiki for her head and chest. One day when R'Kheeya is at her house, she will send a grandchild down for me.

There is talk of snow tomorrow and Monday. Bassam called and asked if I wanted to go out on the donkey tomorrow. I said I would like to go to *Al Barra,* so he is going to leave the donkeys in a cave down at Petra. It is better for them when it is cold.

I did some hand-washing to take advantage of the sun on my door. I sat in the sun and first did the crossword – not very well – and slept on the mattress in the sun. Then Aisha came and just sat by me. I gave her a lovely English/Arabic dictionary with pictures to be looking at but she soon flipped through that and lost interest! At 6.15pm Jasmine came and said that there was no food upstairs – only enough for Bassam's supper. I had a little of the lentil and veg soup left so I cooked some rice flour spaghetti, mixed it all together, and sent it upstairs for Fatma and the children.

17th February. Bassam phoned to say he had to go into Wadi Musa before we could start our ride to *Al Barra.* I said I'd walk down past the *mughur al nazarah,* the "Christian tombs" and meet him down in Petra. They had forecast snow but it was a wonderful morning. When I was away from the village and on my own I took the shawl off my head, but I put it back on again before I got down to Petra. It was good that I did because two mounted policemen came along, took me for a bedouin and didn't ask to see my entrance ticket. [Because I had residency status in Jordan, the cost of entry to Petra was only one dinar, about 80p, as opposed to the tourist price of fifty dinars. It wasn't worth driving into Wadi Musa to buy.]

Bassam soon came with Azuz' replacement, a donkey called Aryan, for me to ride and the mule for himself. As we rode past *Um Al Biyara,* we overtook an old woman who was carrying a heavy bag, so Bassam took her bag and undertook to leave it at the point where we left the track – by Thraya's house. [In fact Thraya was in the village and Bassam had asked Fatma to prepare lunch for her.]

Each time we ride onto *Al Barra* I try to memorize the route but it is very complicated with lots of almost identical places where you need to know the way. I would like to take myself up there one day. There are two places where I have to dismount and Bassam takes the animals a different way, because the route is too difficult for them. There was a glorious view from the top. We could see the smoke from fires in Israel.

We met Bassam's uncle, Ghasm's new young wife. She is sixteen now and pregnant already. She was looking for a goat that they had lost yesterday. We made a fire and cooked chicken on a *shaback* or grid. Delicious. We talked a lot. He told me about a problem with his sister-in-law following his father's death. I explained my money situation to him. I was living on a pension now and needed to be careful. He is going to arrange for the man to come and finish the top of the steps, and to build a wall to the side of my house. I also said that, later on, I would like the garden paved. It is just hard-baked earth at the moment.

On our return to Petra, I waited with Aryan on the bridge while Bassam went to put the mule in the cave. While I was waiting, with the tether in my hand, Aryan started pulling towards another donkey and all but mounted him. I was pulling very hard and was very grateful when a camel man came and helped me. That animal is awful. He always wants to mount any creature be they mule or donkey, male or female, as long as they are smaller than he is. More than once he has tried it, with me on his back!!

When we returned home, Fatma was just about to serve *magloba* to Thraya, two of Thraya's children, her mother, two of her sisters and three of her sister's children, as well as her own children. We joined them. With a full tummy, I went home and slept in the sun. Jasmine came, drank weak coffee and had a welsh cake. She went and returned with her mother. So I made them tea with sage and gave Fatma the rest of the welsh cakes. When they had gone I got the lounge warm and had a strip wash in front of the gas fire. I then rubbed lavender and chamomile oils into my legs, to try to avoid stiffness in my muscles from today's walk and ride.

18th February. Housework first. I needed to use my vacuum cleaner this morning then remembered that Fatma still had it. I saw Chofa. She had popped home in her break from school. I told her I needed the "electric broom" later.

This was followed by a trip to the vegetable market. I gave a lift to Hammad [So'mah's husband.] H'layla [Fatma's sister] appeared from nowhere and climbed in too. I went to my favourite stall in the market. The shop looked very attractive. I told Faras that his shop looked like a picture. I stocked up because snow is forecast for later today and tomorrow.

I had to park my car far away this morning and walk to the Crowne Plaza because the President of Portugal is here and no cars were allowed. The hotel general manager was there with a high-ranking army officer. I showed them Pete's picture. [My son is a Royal Marine] All very impressed!

Home and Ali (Thraya's son) was the first visitor He had come from school coughing and spluttering. Once again, he was wearing just a thin sweater. I asked him where his Government- issue jacket was. [Warm, quilted jackets are distributed to the children by their schools at this time every year. The teachers always explain that the jackets are a personal gift from His Majesty King Abdullah.] At home, he said. [Home is a cave an hour's walk from the school.] I told him that he was foolish and that he ought to be wearing his jacket.

I gave him the leftover half of chocolate bar which Aisha had given me, and a glass of pineapple juice. Then Jasmine and Chofa came and sat in front of the fire, first looking at books then playing with the playing cards. Ali went. They had rice cakes with peanut butter. Aisha came for a while. Supper is at her house tonight – although Fatma will cook it. She said that she wanted to return at 3pm for me to do more Reiki on her. She never returned. Jasmine and Chofa left but Jasmine soon returned with the airtight box I'd used for the Welsh cakes last night. Immediately her mother followed with the "electric broom." Fatma had rice cakes and peanut butter and tea with sage. [I had an unusual accident while I was making it. The water in the teapot came to the boil. I lifted the lid and added the loose tea. When I replaced the lid, it resisted, so I pushed rather too hard. The entire lid went into the pot – edgewise, followed by my hand!! I put it under the cold tap and later put some cream on but it is still burning! Serves me right for not knowing my own strength!]Jasmine stayed and ate one of her mother's rice cakes and drank 3 glasses of tea before I told her to stop to ensure there was enough for her mother to have more. Then Abdullah (Fatma's 5 year old son) arrived. He had a glass of tea. Fatma needed a lemon. Then they all went.

Fatma came down to say that supper was ready at her mother's house. Bassam was already there with Chofa,

Ahmad and Abdullah. Aisha, Hamda's youngest daughter was there with two of her brothers. Hamda has had 14 children; 13 are still alive. Fatma is her fourth child. She brought in a huge platter of *magloba* made with six chickens. When we had all finished eating from the platter, small empty dishes were brought and the leftovers were divided amongst the sisters, to take home to their families. One lot was for H'layla's family. Another was for the absent sons who would eat later. I estimate that 15-16 people would have been fed from that platter.

I stayed a while and drank tea. Bassam reported that the man wanted 40 dinars for doing the steps and wall outside my house. There is a shortage of breeze - blocks at the moment because the weather is not warm enough to dry them off quickly. Bassam thinks the whole job will cost about JD 90. The price of building materials has trebled in the last two years. It is largely because of the influx of wealthy Iraqis who can afford to build huge apartments blocks in Amman. As a result, Amman is quite a boom city but the knock-on effect for the people down here is serious. The Government has also recently removed the subsidy for calor gas bottles. One of my friends who is very pro-Palestinian says that the pro- Jewish International Monetary Fund is insisting that the Jordanian Government does away with all such subsidies. He said that they want to cause unrest. The more unrest there is in the Arab lands of the Middle East, the more secure Israel feels. I do not know enough about it to comment on that line of thought. However, when I mentioned it to Bassam, he said that there was some ill-feeling in the south because the king was often seen on TV giving aid to the country's Palestinians.

19th February. I spent the morning doing domestic things. I vacuumed all the carpets and cooked some chicken and vegetables. It is still very cold and overcast here. I had a text from Edwina, my friend in Amman. She said there was snow and strong winds in Amman and that the schools were shut. Fatma came with Jasmine. She said that the schools here were shut too because there is no means of heating them. I offered the chicken and vegetable I had made for supper tonight but Chofa has already prepared *malfoof* for tonight – a supper to which I am invited. I said that the food I prepared would keep until tomorrow. I made sage tea and gave them a rice cake with peanut butter. If the weather is good, Fatma wants to go to Aqaba tomorrow to see the doctor. She wants to take So'mah, her sister and Chofa, her older daughter, too.

Later. The lobby was full of people from a cruise ship but they returned to their buses soon after I arrived. I told Amjad at the shop that I might be going to Aqaba tomorrow. He advised against going early saying that there might be ice on the road on the high passes. I met Hammad, So'mah's husband on the road as I drove back through the village. He wanted me to go and have tea at his house. I had to explain that I was invited upstairs for *malfoof*.

Jasmine and Ayeesha arrived soon after I returned. I chastised Jasmine for writing on my crossword. She must have done it when I was out in the kitchen getting tea for her and her mother this morning. I told her that she knew that it was wrong otherwise she wouldn't have waited until I was out if the room before doing it. She looked very sheepish. Bassam was invited to supper at Nasser's house but he called to say there wasn't much food there and would there be some *malfoof* left? He must have gone into Wadi Musa later because three of the children came after I had settled for the evening with a piece of gateau that Bassam had bought in the town. I spent the evening doing the Times crossword, reading The Iliad and watching the Kate Beckinsale version of Emma – far preferable in my opinion to the Gwyneth Paltrow one. Fatma is still hoping to go to Aqaba tomorrow if the weather is fine.

20th February. Well, the weather today was what, in the Air Force, we used to call "Harry clampers." In other words, very poor visibility and low cloud. No word from upstairs about the trip to Aqaba. This is wise. It is also likely that the children are home because the schools are closed. The reason for the closures in Amman is because the snow prevents pupils from getting to school. The reason here is because the school is not heated. Some classrooms have a calor gas heater but one of these is not sufficient to heat the room.

So, I had a domestic morning. The airer is in the kitchen but the drying conditions are not good. There is already a lot of condensation on the windows from the gas rings. I may go and visit Abdullah [the night security supervisor at the Crowne Plaza] and his family. He called twice when I was in the UK but I missed the calls and haven't yet made contact.

On the way to Abdullah's in Wadi Musa, I called at the Crowne Plaza for coffee. Ali Salameen came and we talked at some length. He is keen to resume the French classes but not through the language school. Ten minutes after Ali had returned to work, Magedi [from the very same language school] called and I ignored it. Then I bought two dinars' worth of cakes to take to Abdullah's family, alongwith some clothes that Edwina had given me.

The family were very welcoming and delighted to see me and my gifts, but it became an exhausting three hours. I was invited to stay for lunch which they said would be ready in an hour. It took two hours. Then I was offered tea but the kettle was put on the room fire to boil so it took ages! Throughout, the four boys and one girl, all under 11 years, vied for my attention with a loud TV as a backdrop to their performances. I was numb with tiredness when I got home. By then the sun had appeared and I tried to rest in the sunny hallway but first Ayeesha came followed by Jasmine, then their mother, saying that she would like the chicken and vegetables for supper tonight. Then Gasseem's son came to say that Bassam was in Beda with some tourists. Would I please join them?

Fatma and So'mah definitely want to go to Aqaba tomorrow. Judging by tonight's beautiful moon, the weather will be good tomorrow. They want to set off at 7am to be at the doctors when it opens at 9am.

22nd February. Yes, well, yesterday was a day and a half. I'll give an account of it before I get too caught up in today.

I was ready, as planned, at 7am but it was 7.20 before we set off. The skies were clear but the *shergiya* (south wind) was strong. As we drove through Taybeh and rounded a bend on the mountain road, a beautiful sight presented itself. We could see the mountainside clothed in low cloud, not thickly but enough to coat the earth.

Once we drove into it, however, it was not so beautiful: visibility was poor, the vegetation was covered with a heavy frost and the road, in parts, was icy. At one point, I was going downhill and had dropped down into third when a situation developed. The car I had been following stopped rather abruptly in order to let someone out. He stopped opposite another car, parked on the other side of the road. At the bottom of the hill was a left hand bend with two cars parked on it. I needed to brake and did so very carefully. Despite the gentleness of the application, the wheels locked and the car was, in effect, skidding towards the two parked cars. Fatma, who was sitting in the front, realised what was happening. She gasped as I did my best to negotiate the downhill stretch, the two cars and the bend. Fortunately, I succeeded but Fatma was really rattled. Having been so keen to set off early, she wanted to stop at the side of the road and wait for the cloud to lift. I judged that, as long as we went carefully, we would be OK. It was a suggestion she repeated 15 minutes later when the conditions hadn't improved. I said that if she would be happier, I would stop but that I thought we would be fine – so we continued. After ten more minutes we left the low cloud behind, negotiated the highest pass, reached the main road and dropped down the thousand metres to Wadi Rum and Aqaba.

We parked the car near where Fatma thought the doctor's surgery was. However, we walked quite a long way and it became apparent that she was going to need help to find it. The first person she asked just said that it was "Up." I said that I would go back for the car and bring it to where we had got to. I did that, soon found them again and off we went to the doctors. There, we had a two- hour wait before Fatma and So'mah were seen by the doctor. I slept for the first half hour. Another woman from our village came in while we were waiting. Her name was also Fatma. She is the mother of Bassam Ali Salaama, the man whose donkey I rode on when I first came to Petra. She had travelled alone on the 6am bus from Wadi Musa. She was therefore fully covered in a black headdress with just slits for the eyes. There were only ladies in the waiting room, so she lifted up the veil when she was talking to us.

By the time we left the doctors we were all starving. We went to an upstairs restaurant and Fatma Ali (who had been seen first at the doctors) was already there. We ate half a chicken each, rice and okra in a lovely stew. It was decided that Fatma Ali would come back with us in the car.

From the restaurant we went to the souq for the ladies to buy things for the family and their houses. I stayed with them for a while watching them rubbish every price they were offered, making the men empty their stock cupboards and still walking away. As we left one place, I turned and quietly said,

"*Assifah* Sorry."

That shopping took another two hours. Then they wanted to go to the beach. We found a place where I could park the car and we could have access to the public beach. [Not easy in Aqaba where the sea front is owned by hotels and clubs for the wealthy.] We approached a cafe on the beach but Fatma and her sister So'mah were nervous because most of the tables were occupied by men. However I was so desperate for a cup of coffee to keep me awake on the journey home and Fatma Ali was also determined, so the other two were persuaded to join us. Coffees and teas were ordered. Then an unusual thing happened. Fatma Ali, entirely covered again, took her phone out of her bag and started playing music on it, very loudly and instantly drawing the attention of all the surrounding men. Fatma and So'mah looked embarrassed. So, I said to Fatma Ali, apparently jokingly,

"It's all right for you, covered up under all that black. But we are all open!" Everyone laughed. However Fatma Ali was not content with that. She then lifted her *fustan* slightly and rolled up her jeans, preparing to go for a paddle. She is a 46 yr old lady with thirteen children! We stayed at the table while she went off. Fatma was thoroughly embarrassed. I wanted to shout out,

"Good for you, Fatma Ali!"

When she had paddled enough, we left the downtown area and went to a western-style supermarket because I needed groceries that I couldn't buy in Wadi Musa or Um Sayhoun. Such a shop was an eye-opener for the ladies. They said,

"This shop is not for us. It is very expensive." However they did agree that the 3 kilos of sugar that I had bought for JD 1.30 was a good buy. It was only later that it dawned on me that none of those ladies could read, not even the numbers on the price tags.

The rest of the journey home was smooth. Fatma Ali was called several times by her family, wanting to know when she would be back. She was also making the others laugh by saying that she wanted to take a second husband, one for the daytime and one for night time!

As we turned into the oval area where Fatma Ali and So'mah lived, their menfolk were out on the street, waiting to welcome them and to see that they were safely back. I resisted invitations to drink tea. By way of thanks, Fatma Ali had already invited me to supper on the following Saturday.

As we reached home, Bassam called to say that supper was at his mother's house and that we should go directly there. So we unpacked the car and went to H'layla's. R'Kheeya, one of Bassam's sisters, was there with her husband and their baby girl. So too were the two Nassers and Majid and Fatma and two of Wotha's daughters .(Wotha is Bassam's elder sister.)

Supper was chicken *mansaf*. The men ate from one platter and the ladies from another – all in the same room. It was the only one with a fire. When we had finished, Ahmed and Majid (two of Bassam's brothers) arrived. Ahmed is the best educated having a university degree and very good English. He is unmarried at 32 yrs and has had foreign girlfriends. He talks a lot. He likes to isolate me in the company of others by insisting on speaking English to me. Then he started to tease Fatma about the effects of the burns on her face. He turned to me and said,

"I am calling her Japanese because of her slit eyes." I said,

"I know you are. You are not good. You did that before, the very first time I met you three and a half years ago." By then I had risen to go. In doing so, I took hold of R'Kheeya's baby from H'layla, her grandmother. The child was in distress and very windy and H'layla wanted to go off and get some *yansoon* (a kind of aniseed infusion) to settle her tummy. I put her up on my shoulder and put gentle pressure on her front and back and she stopped crying for a while.

As I was leaving, Ahmed said that he wanted to have a big feast out in the desert and wanted to invite me. I explained that I was going to Amman then to Germany from 27th February to the 3rd March. He said that they would postpone it until I could be there.

Once again my ears were ringing with tiredness by the time I reached home. I simply put the shopping away and settled in front of two episodes of Barchester Towers. It really is priceless stuff, despite its comparative age. On several occasions I laughed aloud. I particularly liked the reference to the bill being passed through parliament, concerning the bodily searching of nuns for Jesuitical symbols by elderly Anglican clergymen!

I slept very well and went to the Crowne Plaza for breakfast this morning. Before I went, Aisha came to say that her teacher had cancelled the planned visit to her house in Wadi Musa for extra tuition. Aisha was cross with her but I said that it was better for me because I wanted to wash my hair when the sun comes round on my door. Also I do not know whether or not to expect Jaffar, his mother and sister. I rang last Monday to invite them to visit tomorrow and he said he was going to speak to his mother. I have heard no more. I will send a text later to see what is happening. Jaffar, from a Wadi Musa family, has become a great friend. He first came to my house to install the TV satellite. He has shown me great kindness, even helping me to buy, and then installing, the geyser in the kitchen which supplies all my hot water.

[On the way back from Aqaba yesterday Magedi from the language school called twice. He later sent a text asking if we could meet to discuss doing further French and English courses together. I replied that I was not interested in teaching any more courses for him. I refuse to teach in order to make money for his investors. I didn't tell him that but I will if he pushes me.]

23rd February. Jaffar called to say that his mother's sister had arrived from Ma'an and that they couldn't visit me today. However, I was invited to go to their house for lunch – *magloba* – at 2pm. That gave me time to wash my hair but it meant that I had to dry it in front of the gas fire because the sun was not warm enough.

Fatma came with her prescriptions from Aqaba and the money for the medicines. She asked me to call at the chemist while I was in Wadi Musa. That was no problem. She said that Rabbayah's pick-up had been stolen from outside his house during the night. The police had been informed. (Rabbayah is Wotha's husband.)

I was warmly welcomed at Jaffar's house by his mother, sisters, brothers, aunt and her children. There followed the usual bombardment. The younger sister always wants to talk English but her English really isn't good enough to carry on even a simple conversation. The five-year-old nephew was having fun balancing on the tops of the back cushions. He particularly liked to be in my space. His uncles remonstrated with him but they were ignored and then did nothing. After a while, and fearful of his falling into my lap, I grabbed his hand in such a way that he was forced to climb down. He gave me a very puzzled look - that I should have had the audacity to interfere with his game.

Jaffar explained that, although he had set up a Yahoo mail account he hadn't been able to use it because he couldn't read the messages on the screen. So we all went into what I think is the brothers' sleeping room, where the computer is set up. There are five brothers still at home, with only one married. The family home is an old building high up in the town. Its construction is such that further building on the roof is not possible. So, the place that would have become new homes for the sons as they married, has to remain a flat roof which houses the bread oven and which provides private sitting out space for the sisters.

Jaffar is part of a locally arranged broadband network which allows sharing of the line over 50 metres. We went to Yahoo but he couldn't remember what he had told them before, so we set up a new address. I was able to check my email while I was there too. One of the sisters, the oldest I think, has started working in the kitchens at the hospital. Maria, the next sister down, completed her nursing training last month, but does not seem in a hurry to get herself registered and to start work. She has dreams of working in the Gulf or furthering her studies in the UK. I suggested that it would be better for her to get work experience in Jordan first. She seemed disappointed with that idea but Jaffar agreed with me.

The lunch was served at 4pm. Three or four platters had to be prepared and placed in different rooms because of the number of people. I ate with Jaffar, Mousa, Omar, Maria, the aunt and two of her children. It was tasty but not as good as Fatma's (or indeed mine.) Part of the problem was that it was luke-warm. The other is that I think that the chicken had been pre-cooked and not boiled in with the rice, stock and spices. It was therefore not very tender and needed quite a lot of chewing. After some time, tea was served. Having been there for three hours, I felt that I could take my leave. Where are you going? Why are you going? Our house is your house. I said that I had two reasons for going. i) I had been there 3 hours and was now tired. ii) I had medicine for Fatma and wanted to get it to her.

Once again, I was numb with fatigue. I came home, read The Iliad and dozed. Fatma came down and I gave her the medicine. She asked me if I wanted to eat supper with them. I explained that I had eaten lunch very late but that I would like to come up for tea after they had eaten.

When I went up later, I discovered that Bassam had gone down to Wadi Araba with some of the other men, to look for Rabbayah's car. I stayed and watched a TV programme with Fatma and the children. For my benefit, they had selected the Discovery Channel. It was about lions in Africa, with an English commentary. There was a part where the lion was showing interest in the lioness. I couldn't resist translating the fact that they sometimes make love as often as 40 times a day. I heard the children repeat "40 times a day" with wonderment. I smiled at Fatma and said "That's a good idea" and she giggled. A bit later the commentary explained that the lioness certainly makes it known when she is not interested. So I translated that the lioness could say No. I turned to Fatma again and said "That's another good idea!" Her reaction was similar, but this time accompanied by a knowing look.

I finished watching the Barchester Chronicles which was wonderful, but then I had difficulty sleeping. I think that I was overtired. It took me ages to get to sleep and I awoke late this morning – 8.20. Jasmine was soon at my door explaining that we were going to Beda today to see the big goats' hair tent that Bassam has bought from his brother Sa'ood. Sa'ood's idea had been to keep chickens there and sell the eggs but he has been without his car since last November. It has been up in Amman. It was now ready for collection and he needed some money to go and reclaim it. Sa'ood is Bassam's half brother, their father's oldest son by a long-dead wife. He is Thraya's full brother. He does not own his own home and was 36 yrs before he married. His 20 yr old wife, Hasseena, is expecting their second child.

Bassam found Rabayyah's car in Wadi Finan. It had been taken by two of Zaynab's sons. (She is Fatma's oldest sister and the mother of the afflicted Faisal of chapter 1.) I will find out more when I go out to the tent. Bassam phoned to say that all the family were going out to their land, to kill a goat and give thanks for the return of the car. I explained that I needed to be back to accept Fatma Ali's invitation to have supper with her. I will go when I have finished this and made some inquiries about a Syrian visa. I have been invited to go up to Damascas for a couple of days when I return from Germany. I have also received an invitation to Ken and Sandra's farewell do at the Grenadiers next Wednesday. Since that is the night before I fly to Germany, I shall be in Amman and able to attend.

I had to leave the car down on the road to get to the family encampment at *Shemazza*. The recent rain had carved channels too deep for my car. The walk to their tent took me 25 minutes. Jasmine was looking out for me. It's a wonderful place; high and against a flat carved rock face. The tent is new and long and is surrounded by a fence. Fatma was making *mukhdooda* (frying the goat's liver and kidneys with onions.) H'layla was there and Ahmad (R'Kheeya's husband). Majid came later from *Al Deir* where he and Ahmed have the shop they bought from Sa'ood. I stayed a couple of hours and left in order to have a rest before having supper at Fatma Ali's. They were making *magloba* with the goat's meat.

After the welcome rest, I donned traditional Bedouin dress and I set off to Fatma Ali's. She was looking out for me from her flat roof- top. I was greeted by some of her family on the terrace. Her husband was there and recognised me from several meetings on the *mughur al nasara* road. They have thirteen children: eight girls and five boys. There is only one son left at home and he is engaged. There are six girls still at home. After we had eaten, Bassam Ali Salaama (their oldest son) arrived. He had come to invite me to dine at his house tomorrow.

After tea I got up to leave. Fatma gave me a lovely red and black fustan and her older daughter went to Sudani's shop with me to buy some *kohl* eye liner. I had noticed the beautiful effect on Fatma's eyes in Aqaba, after she had lifted her veil!

24th February. A quiet start to the day. Warmer, so the strip- wash from a bowl in front of lounge fire was not too fierce an experience. There was an email from Magedi, hoping that we could be "partners" when / if I feel like resuming the French. I replied, wishing him and his family well but ignoring the proposition.

I made soup, washed the car and settled to the crossword before having a rest. Ten minutes later Fatma appeared asking if we could take Jasmine to the hospital. She had been helping her mother with the goats in their pens when she had fallen from a height onto a breeze-block wall. Her arm certainly didn't look right. The drive to the hospital took 25 minutes. An X-ray revealed that she had a bad break to her right arm, above the elbow. A Russian doctor took charge of her case. How she howled when he expertly yanked the bones back into position. She had two further x-rays to ensure that the bones were lined up correctly before plastering. He wants to see her again on Tuesday.

We went straight to the chemist to get some pain-killing syrup and then to the dessert shop. I went in while Fatma stayed in the car with Jasmine. Fatma wanted a dinar's worth of cakes. I thought the tray he was using was very small. It became clear that he was trying to cheat me out of the correct number of cakes. I said,

"I bought 2 dinars' worth the other day. You are giving me less than half of that. "The shop was filling but I stuck to my guns. He weighed the tray and said,

"How about 60p?" I said,

"I didn't ask for 60p's worth. I asked for a dinar's worth. I am speaking Arabic well. You are not listening well." The other customers, all male, thoroughly enjoyed my joke. I said,

"Use a bigger tray." I prevailed in the end.

When Jasmine was settled at home, I had a half hour's rest before going to Bassam Ali Salaama's for supper. As usual I was very well received. He has a lovely family. Five children, three girls and twin boys. One of the boys was asleep the whole time under a blanket. He has trouble with both eyes apparently and has to visit hospital frequently. Supper was *mansaf* with chicken, with Bassam Ali kindly picking the chicken off the bone for me and dropping it on my segment of the platter. Tea and then home but not before I had resisted an invitation to stay and sleep there! [Bassam told me that Rabbayah is asking for JD 1000 in compensation for his car being taken: JD 500 from Khaled and JD 500 from his brother. Apparently they have agreed. This is because damage was done to the engine when they took it and repairs are going to cost at least that.

25th February. Today started very gently and quietly but then became rather complicated – as is often the case here.

I slept well until 8am. (It's so much easier to sleep in the winter months.) I made breakfast and took it back to bed while I watched the BBC World news. Fatma came while I was doing that and wanted to borrow the vacuum cleaner. Bassam has gone to Amman today with Nasser, for the latter to see a doctor about a problem with his nose. When I had tidied, I went to the Crowne Plaza and, on the way, gave Jasmine, the patient, some sultanas. I brought a cake back for her and she shared it with Chofa. While I was at their house, the heavens opened with heavy rain, thunder and lightning. The wadi bottom was awash. At one very loud thunder clap, the electricity was cut. When I returned to my house, I found rainwater running down the wall under the window on the exposed side, and the seating mattresses there sodden. I put towels in place but had to keep an eye on them for the rest of the day. Fortunately I sleep under the window on the non-exposed side but I nevertheless pulled my sleeping mattress well out from the wall.

Later, when I had had some lunch, Fatma came down. She had been with the goats. Their shelter was full of water. There were four new kids. She had some lentil soup and we discovered that the electricity had returned to her house, but not to mine. So, I phoned Jaffar. He was very busy moving all his stuff from his former shop, but he phoned his brother, Jebreen, who is an engineer at the Crowne Plaza. He came within 15 minutes with another man. They quickly solved the problem, which they explained to me. Unfortunately my Arabic was not nearly good enough to understand the technicalities.

With the electric problem sorted, I wanted to go back to the Crowne Plaza to post my cards and to get some gifts from Amjad's shop to take to Mechthild's family on my German visit.

Bassam and Nasser are still in Amman, waiting to see a doctor. Their brother Khalil had supper with us. I had made some welsh cakes. The children were generally good about sharing them. They are being kind to Jasmine, the wounded soldier. I shall be taking her and Fatma back to the hospital tomorrow morning.

26th February. I am writing this at 7.50 pm at the end of another tiring day. An hour and a half of this morning was spent at the hospital with Fatma and Jasmine. Another x-ray was taken and showed the bones to be lined up very well.

After that we went into town. I bought a chicken and some vegetables for supper, having offered to prepare tonight's *magloba* for the family. Bassam is still in Amman. Fatma bought chicken *shwarma* (a fast-food roll) for lunch. I settled down for a rest but only got an hour before Chofa and Jasmine came down. Then it was time to start cooking the supper.

I am off to Amman tomorrow. I will stay at Edwina's and attend Ken's party in the evening. Off to Dusseldorf on Thursday until Monday.

So ended my journal. I think that it helped my friends to gain some understanding of the rhythm of life in Um Sayhoun. More than that, it also helped them to realise why I could only answer their questions in sound-bites. Living the very life was quite enough, without either reliving it in a journal at the end of each day or trying to give accounts of it in the occasional telephone calls.

Chapter 11
On Delicate Ground

As I discovered on my trip to the *hujamah* with Thraya, traditional medicine was popular. It was cheap and the people had great faith in it. Surprisingly, both to me and to my neighbours, I myself was to introduce a different kind of traditional healing. In the same way that there are plants to help combat the world's illnesses, there is also a readily available source of 'electrical' healing energy. Reiki. The dynamic that this introduced into my relationships with the Bedouin reveals a lot about their openness on the one hand, and the constraints under which they live on the other.

Five years before my first visit to Jordan, I had attended a symposium in Milan at which His Holiness the Dalai Lama was present. I was the guest of two gay Italian friends; one I had known for a year, the other I was meeting for the first time. The new acquaintance is a Reiki Master. On the second day, he said to me,

"Ah…Joanna, you have such strong energy. You must let me do a Reiki attunement on you." I knew little about Reiki but, given the backdrop of saffron-clothed monks and their tantric chanting, my heart and mind were open to anything that felt right. This did. So, Sergio gave me a Level 1 attunement and, six months later on my second visit, he attuned me to the second level.

I told no one else what had happened and lived privately with these attunements for seven years. That is, until the summer of my retirement from the International Community School in Amman and my imminent move to the Bedouin village.

I was in England in August of that year, 2006, and had met a friend for coffee. She was worried about her daughter, a beautiful twenty-year-old, who was reading Natural Sciences at Oxford. Her life was being blighted by ulcerative colitis. The May balls had been agony, with her beautiful dresses concealing sanitary towels and cycling shorts in order to prevent an accident. He mother said,

"I am desperate, Joan, she is on the strongest possible medication. I am seriously considering something like acupuncture or Reiki." My heart lurched as it does when I feel that I am being given a signal for action.

"Ah," I said, "did I ever tell you that I have a second level Reiki attunement?" [I knew that I hadn't, because I hadn't told anyone.]

"Oh, Joan, have you? That's wonderful. I would be really shy about suggesting such a thing to my daughter but I know that she loves and trusts you." The die was cast. Her daughter called me later that evening and an appointment was made for her to come to my house on the following day. In the meantime, I was desperately seeking out my books and notes in order to prepare myself for the session. I was truly nervous, venturing onto such uncharted territory but, when the moment came, I was strangely calm and confident. All went well.

Two days later, the young woman called to arrange another session. The day before her first visit, she had opened her bowels ten times; the day following, she had been twice. She truly felt helped and planned to seek out a

Reiki practitioner on her return to Oxford. Two days later, I flew out to Amman to take up permanent residence.

Before driving south, I stayed the night with an English friend and her family in Amman. We were chatting quietly about recent events and the huge undertaking that I was about to embark on. She had her feet up on a stool. I asked if she had a problem with her feet. She said,

"No. It's the outside of my left knee. I have been to three different doctors, rubbed in all sorts of cream and there's still no improvement. I have heard that there's a woman on the other side of the town who does Reiki. I might go to her." Once again my heart leapt. Once again, I said,

"Did I ever tell you that I have a second level Reiki attunement?"

"Oh, Joan, that's wonderful. Can we do it now?" The following morning she got out of bed and walked to her bathroom before realizing that the movement had been accomplished without pain, for the first time in weeks. I played it down rather but, as I made the three –hour drive down the Desert Highway, my mind was working overtime.

"Why?" I thought, "After seven years of nothing, why have these two situations arisen within four days of each other? Something is going on here. I must be on the lookout. I must be brave enough to be ready.

During my first two weeks in my new home, at least three different women asked me for strong pain-killing tablets from England.

"*Fee haboob?* Have you got any tablets?" One woman, Fatma's sister Fatma, came more than once. On her third visit, I plucked up courage and said,

"All these tablets aren't good for you, you know. If you want, I could do something else. It is like the Amareen but without the fire." [There is a traditional medicine woman in the Amareen community along the Wadi Araba road. She sometimes applies hot metal and sometimes the glowing end of a herbal cigarette.] "It is not from me. It is from God. *Kullshee min Allah.* Everything is from God."

"*Shoo?* What is it?" she asked.

"Well," I said "I just tune in to some healing energy and I put my hands on you. It is like holding your spectacles in the sun and seeing the heat underneath them. You can bring a friend if you want to." The next day she returned alone, unannounced, and said,

"I want your hands on me." Over the next four months, at least ten women came to my house. I went to their houses. I went to their caves, including Thraya's where her children swung on a corrugated iron door, making a terrible noise throughout. I visited her neighbour's cave. Everywhere the sweat would trickle down my back and down my nose as I tried to kneel on the hard floor, sometimes for as long as half an hour. It was agony.

One day I was paying Thraya a social visit when a neighbour arrived with her husband. He wanted the same as the women. He lay down and approximately four women and six children took up their ringside seats to watch. No pressure there! When I had finished, he said,

"How do you do that?" I replied.

"I don't do it. It is from Allah." Needless to say, I never made a charge but I was rarely at home for my evening meal, having been invited to many suppers by way of thanks.

At the beginning of November, Bassam bought a new camel to work at Petra. It cost him JD 4,000 (about £3,500.) About two weeks later, Bassam explained that he wasn't happy with the camel. He was too slow and could hardly get up the hill to the village. I was concerned for him, and the camel, but thought no more of it. In the second week of

December and three days before I was due to fly back to the UK for Christmas, I was having supper upstairs with Bassam and his family. Bassam said,

"I am going to sell the camel for meat. He is not eating well and he is still very slow."

"How much will you get for that?" I asked.

"Maybe JD 600." Fatma was sitting with us. She had had some Reiki, as had Jasmine and H'layla, Bassam's mother. It was a delicate situation. I said,

"Have the ladies told you about how I've been helping them? It is like the Amareen but without fire." His head quickly swung around to Fatma's face. Unintelligible words passed between them. He looked up at me quietly. I said,

"It works on animals too, you know." That was enough for him. He went to fetch the camel.

I, with heart pounding, washed my hands and crossed my hands on my chest as I started to open the channel. Bassam had the camel near the wall to Gasseem's house, holding tight to his head. It was an enormous animal. I wanted to start on his head. It was all I could do to reach it. I then put my hands on his neck, then between his front legs, then on the side of his stomach. I was about to follow the digestive tract along. However, the camel, judging that I was getting too close to his private parts, lifted a back leg and took a warning swing in my direction. Not being a fool, I decided that I had gone far enough that side and went around to the other side, gingerly giving his hind quarters a wide berth. I started at the head again and, this time, stopped before my hand-positioning became an issue.

That was that. The next night, I said to Bassam,

"Do you want me to do another burst?"

"What do you think?" he replied.

"Well," I said, "you have nothing to lose. It isn't costing you anything and I go to the UK for Christmas the day after tomorrow." He agreed. I repeated the process.

On the third night, having finished eating, we were sitting around a wood fire on Bassam's terrace. Suddenly, Bassam said,

"The camel is well and strong."

"How do you know?" I asked.

"Abdullah, who looks after him for me, says he is eating well, that he is faster and that he very quickly came up to the village after work."

"*Al hamdu lillah.* Thank God," I said. I think I was thinking more of averting the financial loss to Bassam rather than worrying about my own ego.

"Well…do you want me to do a final burst before I travel?" He did.

As I started to put my hands on the camel, I became aware that Bassam's friends, Nasser and Jebreel, were standing in the shadows, watching. Not realizing that I understood what they were saying, they started to talk quietly to Bassam.

"Ah….just putting her hands on. Is that all she does?"

"Yeah," said Bassam, "after she has spoken to her heart." Silence. I moved around to the other side.

"Ah…she's going to the other side," said Nasser. "I thought she'd go to the other side." I blessed the darkness that hid the grin on my face.

When I returned after Christmas, the requests for Reiki decreased. I do not know whether word had spread to the Imam and that he had let it be known that it wasn't a good idea. Only the old women remained faithful and those with a desperate need. Some months after, I caught the tail-end of a conversation that Bassam was having with a friend.

"Well I tell you this. If any of my animals get ill, I am bringing them to Joanna.

I went on to take a third level Reiki and to become a Reiki Master.

Chapter 12
On Being Male

To be born male in this society and, indeed, in the whole of Jordan is to be born into a life of privilege, extraordinary freedom, social supremacy and family responsibilities. A first-born son will give his father a new name. What is more, his birth will give his mother a socially acceptable identity. I was never aware of this among the Bedouin but, in the neighbouring town of Wadi Musa, the men of some family groups would never tell you the name of their fiancées or wives until a son had been born. Then the father would be proud to announce that his wife's name was *Um Omar,* mother of Omar.

Older sisters share the care of the child with his mother. Gradually, as the boy grows, he becomes aware of his privileged status so that even the greater age of his sisters counts for nothing in the face of his natural authority. I have seen boys as young as four or five enter a room and bark at their sisters,

"Jib myah. Bring me water." Most girls grumble and initially refuse but the coaxing of the parents ensures that the water is fetched. If the girls are unusually determined, the mother rises and fetches the water. The husbands allow this.

127

When a boy is old enough to go to school, he will spend his first year or two in a special classroom at the Girls' School. The atmosphere there is kinder with the risk of bullying and violence in the playground removed. He will also go home earlier before the older boys are on the streets. In Um Sayhoun, the Boys' School lies behind a high wall close to the main road through the village. At any time during the school day, sounds of shouting and screeching furniture can be heard from the road. I never entered the Boys' School but I am quite sure that most of the teachers, all male, carried sticks to ensure discipline.

Bassam was one of six brothers. Only one of them wanted to continue his education past the school leaving age. To do this, he had to attend school in the neighbouring town. At that time, there was no bus service, so he lived with a family in Wadi Musa. He later read archaeology at the University of Jordan and became a tour guide.

To my knowledge, none of the teachers in the Boys' School were from Um Sayhoun. However, one of Bassam's uncles was the headmaster of the Boys' School in the neighbouring village of the Amareen.

For many boys, and their fathers, education was something that had to be lived through, rather than valued. The school attendance record of most teenage boys was poor. Some would divide their week between school and Petra. As soon as their fathers allowed it, they preferred to be working with tourists on the family donkeys. They seemed to get away with it. Their fathers would go to the police station in Wadi Musa, give some reason for the boys to work and all would be well.

Toys were almost unknown in the Bedouin village. If a father returned from a trip to Amman or Aqaba, he might bring a Made-in-China plastic car or dumper truck. The life of such things was, not surprisingly, very short. The boys preferred to be out and about, being mischievous.

I only once saw Bassam punish one of his sons. The boy had poured fruit juice over another boy's head. In a very short time, the boy's head was black with flies and he went home crying to his mother. She came to remonstrate with Fatma. I say that she came but, in fact, she stopped between two neighbouring houses ten metres away, behind a breeze-block wall and shouted her complaint to Fatma so that all the neighbours could hear. The culprit quickly disappeared during the woman's tirade but, when Bassam returned home that evening, he was informed, caught the boy and spanked him.

This same son, the youngest and most indulged, was a hero in his set for his audacity. I was standing at the main road one day, waiting to guide to my house, some friends who were paying their first visit. I was facing the road and had my back to the narrow streets. Suddenly, I felt a stinging slap on my bottom that absolutely took my breath away. I turned to see Abdullah running away. He was seven years old at the time and I was sixty three.

The traditional tasks of the Bedouin male were to find water and wood, feed and pasture for his animals and a place of safety for his family. His life was lived in the mountains. His wife remained at home raising his family, weaving goats' hair, making cheese and yoghurt from the goats' milk and keeping his tent, tomb or cave as clean as she could in the arid conditions.

With the construction of Um Sayhoun, there was no longer any need to find water and fuel or a place of safety. In the recent years of drought, the government even provided an allocation of animal feed for each family, according to the number in the herd. The tourist work in Petra occupied the men for most of the day. A man's favourite social activity was with other men. Often, after work, they would go into the mountains and cook their supper in traditional ways; sometimes *muchmara* a wonderful chicken dish cooked in a hole in the ground, or a barbecue cooked on a piece of metal grill. It seemed to me that there was a great sense of closeness. Most barbers shops were called 'The Brothers'.

Do-it-yourself or tools did not feature in these men's lives. If there was a problem in the maintenance of the home, the women were expected to try and make the repair. The women, were, indeed, very resourceful and could manage many things. If, however, the problem was beyond them, then their husbands would arrange for an Egyptian labourer to come and sort it out.

If the home was the domain of the women, then all public places belonged to the men. A Bedouin woman would try not to walk on the main street, preferring to take parallel back streets. In the village shops, a woman would expect to be ignored if a man was waiting to be served, or to have her transaction interrupted if a man had entered the shop after her. Having said that, the situation in Um Sayhoun was much better than in other parts of Jordan.

I was once in a currency exchange shop in Amman. My transaction was being dealt with and the man behind the counter was mid-sentence in addressing me. A man entered the shop, stood too close to me and shouted his demand across me. I expected the worker to indicate that he was busy with me. When he didn't, I took a step back from the man and said,

"Will you please wait? I am trying to do business here." He laughed and began a catalogue of profuse, grotesque apologies. His performance did not prevent my seeing that my request produced an audible gasp from the six or seven exchange workers, seated at desks behind the counter. To a man, their heads shot up like a group of basking seals who suddenly scent danger. A manager appeared from the back, took over my transaction and allowed the man who had been serving me to see to the demanding new customer.

On another occasion I was in a small shop in Wadi Musa. Again, I was at the counter, being served. A car drew up outside and two young men entered the shop. They behaved as if I wasn't there. One took a carton of juice from a fridge and plonked it on the counter right in front of me. The other went into the interior of the shop, returned with his goods and promptly stretched across me, all but touching my breasts with his forearm as he placed his purchases at an unnecessarily great distance. I simply stood and watched the performance. Their transaction done, they noisily returned to their car, laughing and joking as they looked back over their shoulders to see the effect of their performance. I followed them with my eyes. One had the grace to look somewhat cowed when he saw the look of disgust and contempt on my face. The young man behind the counter, who had served me very nicely on several previous occasions, was completely mortified and simply couldn't meet my eyes.

It was a matter of great pride to the men folk that all problems could be settled within the community, without any outside involvement. When the Bedouin were first moved from their tombs and caves into the village, there was a police station with officers drawn from other parts of Jordan, resident in Um Sayhoun. Some years before I started to live in the village, there had been a tragic event which brought that arrangement to an end. The story went that some young men had started to build a house on a piece of land owned by the father of one of them. The police doubted the ownership of the land and, when the men refused to stop building, the police arranged for bulldozers to be brought in to raze the structure to the ground.

The young men were warned of the approach of the heavy plant and went to the site to try to stop what was happening. In the melee that ensued the police opened fire killing three of the young men. One of them was Bassam's older brother Abdullah, who was shot in the throat. His Majesty King Hussein himself came to the village. He confirmed that the men had the right to build and he sent all the police away. Thereafter, it was left to the elders of the community to sort their problems out. There was always the tourist police in Petra itself and the gendarmerie in Wadi Musa for serious infringements of the law.

Boys are hardened against violence from the moment they can walk. I have seen a father slap his son's face hard to test his reaction. The boy's diaphragm lurched at the shock of the blow and the emotional hurt of being struck by his father. The boy quickly learned not to react, but merely to smile at his triumph of control. On many occasions, if I had cause to intervene in any bad behaviour, my irritation and anger were always compounded by the laughing reaction.

In any society that I am familiar with, there are unwritten and unspoken rules which govern the movement of pedestrian traffic. As you walk along a road, your peripheral vision helps you judge who has the greater right to a narrowing space or to the line being followed. Not so in Jordan. Men and boys expect women to cede the path in any circumstances. Several times, whether I was walking along the road or wandering through Petra on a Friday when most visitors are Jordanian or from the Gulf, this expectation became clear to me. Boys, to whom no rules applied, would drift from their path in such a way that their line would intersect mine. I always held my line. When a boy became aware that his expectation was not being met, he would recoil as from a red-hot poker.

One of the biggest eyesores in the village is the skeleton of the children's playground, which lies on the main road, clearly visible to all the passing tourist buses. There are uprights but no swings. There are bases but no roundabouts or see-saws. There are bench legs but no seats.

The Girls' School overlooks the playground. One of the teachers told me that she had watched from her classroom as the government workers constructed the playground. On the last morning, the finishing touches were added. There were palm trees to provide shade and colourful accessories to make the rides attractive. Within two hours of the workers leaving, the bell of the Boys' School sounded, signaling home-time. The boys fell upon the playground like soldier ants, breaking everything in sight and dismantling all that their bare hands could manage. Everything that could be taken, was taken. None of the boys, or their families, would have had any use for the materials gained. The game was who could get the most. Once away from the play area, their prizes were simply discarded in the road, on the pavements and on the hillsides.

This lack of community spirit or communal pride was general. Litter was scattered everywhere. Most boys would drop sweet wrappers or empty crisp bags first, in the home where their mothers would pick them up, then out on the street where a small army of Egyptian migrant workers did the job. There were about fifty thousand Egyptians working in Jordan. They stayed in the country for nine months of the year and went home for the other three months, usually leaving their wives pregnant and a new child to look forward to the next time. The jobs most of them did were the ones that Jordanian men were too proud to do; street cleaning, sewage repairs, dead animal disposal, labouring on building sites. Their eyes were never available for contact. They worked heads down – except for one man. Whether I was driving, on mule-back or walking on the street, he was always ready and pleased when I waved or greeted him. On my return from a holiday in England, he positively beamed, delighted at my return.

Given such a boyhood and adolescence with so little paternal intervention and with an assumption of male dominance, it was very difficult to see how any young man could reach adulthood with any sense of responsibility, accountability or a balanced view of the relationship between men and women. If they did something naughty or if a complaint was made against them, their father or an uncle would always 'make it better' by providing an excuse or by lying about the boy's involvement or, ultimately, by paying compensation. In the absence of an agreed set of values or a civic conscience, a community needs to find ways of exercising control. In Um Sayhoun, as in the whole of Jordan, one of these mechanisms was family pressure.

Most parents in the village provide each of their sons with a house, usually built onto or above the family home. Once a boy reaches his mid-teens, his parents start to build his house. Following his engagement, the kitchen and bathroom are tiled, the windows put in and all made ready.

If his eye lighted on a girl and his father approved, the father or an uncle would visit the girl's house to talk to her father. If an agreement were reached, the engagement party or *khatbah* would soon follow. These were important social events, especially for the women and girls. There was strict segregation of the sexes. The girls were allowed to be uncovered and, following visits to the salon where their hair and make-up were done professionally, they all looked like princesses. Even the matrons let their hair down on these occasions. I am sure that they felt good in themselves but they were also very aware that, after the party when everyone returned home, the girls would tell their brothers who were the most beautiful young women. Those reports would certainly influence a man's choice of bride.

This system ensured the continuance of the extended family. The bride would be brought to her husband's home, in close proximity to his parents and his brothers' families. Marrying early was encouraged. Most men are married by their early twenties and are quickly thereafter fathers. A long lifetime of providing for their families and their elderly parents would begin.

The other effective mechanism of control is fear. I believe that this is why the most stable Arab countries are either dictatorships or absolute monarchies. Given their nurture, very few Jordanian men will do anything that they don't want to do unless they are afraid. The police, usually drawn from other parts of the country, are respected and obeyed. The *muhabbarat* or plain-clothes police, are a constant presence.

In addition, there is the fear associated with trying to be a 'good Muslim,' as interpreted by the local Imams. In Um Sayhoun, only the Friday prayers attracted a large number of worshippers, all male. There was always a faithful core who attended at least twice daily but, otherwise, mosque attendance was less popular in the village than in Wadi Musa. Even without attendance, the teachings of the Imam had great influence in the village. If a man was going to pray within the following hour, he would not shake a woman's hand. Instead, he would offer the whole of his forearm, covered with a sleeve, by way of greeting.

Very often in shops, the man behind the counter would ensure that his hand didn't touch mine when I offered the money or waited for change. If I offered a note, most men would take it with their fingertips to lessen the danger of physical contact. Or, if the change were several coins, they would be placed down on the counter for me to have to gather up or dropped from an unnecessarily great height into my waiting palm.

Anything which went against the teaching was said to be *haraam*, forbidden. Such strictures pervaded people's lives and the faithful tried very hard to live up to the standards required. The effects of such efforts often created feelings of nervousness, if not fear. A female colleague at the school in Amman had been married to a Jordanian for thirty five years. She was from Manchester and, when they were back visiting family, her husband was very happy to take her arm as they walked around the shops. At their home in Amman, things were very different. After supper one evening, she and her husband were walking on the land at the back of their house. She stumbled and automatically put her hand on her husband's arm to steady herself.

"Don't do that," her husband said, backing off. "What will the neighbours think?"

The arrangement of houses in Um Sayhoun and the poor building fabric of the dwellings were such that nothing was private. As I became established in the village and my opinion respected, I occasionally commented,

"You are not afraid of your God. You are afraid of your neighbours." This was usually met with knowing nods, but silence.

The tension created by the nurture of the men on the one hand and their desire to be good Muslims on the other, was apparent everywhere; not least in the home. A man needed his wife and post-pubescent daughters to cover their hair with *hijabs* and to be dressed in shapeless, loose-fitting clothes with only hands and faces visible. Yet many – in the presence of all their family – would change TV channels to watch American All-In wrestling with the attendant bikini-clad beauties. There was no sense of 'see what degradation our way of life protects us from.' It was purely and simply for the entertainment value, not to say the novelty.

The mix of family control, the fear of mosque and state and the restrictions on social interaction can cause a built-up of testosterone in Arab youth. Flirting with speed and danger can act as safety valves. Among the Bedouin, this took the form of donkey racing or performing dare-devil balancing acts on rock pinnacles (or the urn atop the Monastery monument above Petra.) In wealthier Arab communities racing fast cars (be it in the desert or on the streets of London in the early hours) can also provide some kind of outlet. I wonder too whether the readiness to leave home and country, to go and fight for jihad wherever the struggle is taking place, is driven in part by the need for danger and excitement.

Most men, however, did all they could for their families. They worked to provide income, they did most of the food shopping in Wadi Musa, they bought new clothes for their children at the great festival of *Eid,* they took care of their elderly parents, they tried to help their brothers if they fell on hard times and they attempted to lead upright lives. All of that is, of course, to be applauded. What was more difficult to live with was that, as a result of their nurture, they expected to get their way in all things. If thwarted, their reactions were often violent; first violence of language, then maybe the use of sticks or stones and even, when available, knives and guns. As far as women are concerned, there was an underlying assumption of their own superiority supported by the expectation of their community that they would, at all times, occupy a position of dominance.

Chapter 13
Majid's Story

Majid, one of Bassam's younger brothers, was in his early twenties when I first met him. Occasionally, Bassam and I did a particularly long ride, through Wadi Sabra, the ancient southern approach to Petra, to Taybah Zeiman on the mountain road to Aqaba. It was a climb of some three hundred metres from the wadi bottom up to the village – a punishing climb for us all but particularly for the mules. Majid would drive Bassam's pick-up down a rocky track to a point which was a third of the way out. With great skill, he and Bassam would coax the animals into the back of the pick-up. In normal circumstances, this would have been a very tricky operation, but I have no doubt that the animals were all too aware of the alternative.

Two or three years then passed before I had any further contact with Majid. By that time, he was married to Toba, a well educated woman who had worked as a nurse, and had a son called Ziad. The talk among the women was that, on their wedding night, Majid went through his wife's wardrobe and threw out 90% of her clothes, judging them to be insufficiently shapeless, or too colourful. He always reprimanded his nieces if their cardigans or jackets were unbuttoned, even if they were entirely covered beneath the outer garment.

As a baby, his son suffered from colic and cried a lot. Toba was very patient and tried to give the child to Majid as often as she could in the child's moments of quiet, so that he could enjoy his son at his best. Several times I saw Ziad start to cry when in his father's arms. Majid's response was to make a fist and wave it in the face of his baby son. It was the talk of the family that he had once become so drunk that he grabbed his mother by throat and his brothers had to restrain him by tying his hands together. His wife returned to her father's house that night and stayed there for a week.

My first clash with Majid occurred at the home of a neighbour, Gasseem, a half brother of H'layla and an uncle to Bassam and his siblings. Gasseem was celebrating the new floor tiles in his back yard and had slaughtered three goats for the *mansaf* that would feed his family and friends. When I arrived at sunset, dressed traditionally out of courtesy and in order to identify with the women, the men were sitting in the yard on the new tiles and the women were seated in the main room indoors. A huge pot – maybe a foot deep and two and a half feet in diameter – was on the fire.

The women were sitting around three sides of a square, the door to the yard occupying the fourth side. There were twelve to fifteen women so seated with a dozen children between them; some were sitting quietly by their mothers, others were active and demanding to be entertained. I sat between the two grandmothers – H'layla and Hamda, Fatma's mother, – on the side facing the door. There was some milling in and out but, apart from when they brought the platters of food, the men stayed outside.

We were waiting for the food to arrive when Majid came in. He attracted the attention of Yasmeen, his brother Nasser's daughter, who was nearly two years old. She went to him and he promptly instructed her to strike her mother, indicating his expectation by demonstrating with his own fist. Muna, Yasmeen's mother and one of the best educated women in the village, having spent some time in Bahrain where her father was serving in the Jordanian army, saw what was happening and directed her attention to Yasmeen. She wagged her finger and said,

"*La.La*. No. No." Yasmeen obeyed her and Majid left.

Ten minutes later, Majid re-entered. This time he had Ziad with him. Fatma, Bassam's wife, was sitting on the end of one of the sides. Majid had the attention of the whole room. He took Ziad's hand and was encouraging him to hit Fatma on the shoulder. I could contain myself no longer. I said loudly,

" *Hathee fuckert kwayez* ? Is that a good idea?" I had hardly finished the sentence when Majid stood upright, turned his back and left the room, to the sound of laughter from his mother, his sister, his wife and two of his sisters-in-law. As he retreated I added,

"Ah....so it wasn't a good idea after all." I turned and asked Hamda "That's right, isn't it?"

"*Aywah!* Absolutely", she replied.

It was the first time that I had spoken out in such a way and I wasn't certain what the response of the other women would be. I dropped my head slightly, withdrawing behind the parapet as it were, and glanced quickly at their faces. Most looked at me in admiration. Such a response was, of course, not my purpose, but their looks did indicate that I had done something that they felt required courage. It was clear to me that such a rebuke, from a woman to a man – mild though I considered it – was almost unheard of. My position had been strengthened by the fact that he was on our territory, in the women's room. Fatma later told me that Majid's breath smelled of *arak*.

Some months later, I received one of many invitations to eat my supper upstairs with the family. Two of Bassam's brothers, Nasser and Majid, and his friend, Jebreel, had come to share the food. At a family meal such as that, the men and the women ate together. During the meal, Majid asked Bassam where Jasmine was. She was by then thirteen years old and, being post-pubescent, covered her head. She had severe learning difficulties and had stopped going to school.

I could see that Bassam was embarrassed that he couldn't account for her whereabouts. Towards the end of the meal, she appeared.

"Where have you been?" her father asked sharply.

"At my grandmother's," she replied. Hamda's house was just three doors away.

"You are always at your grandmother's. I am sick of hearing that you are at your grandmother's." I think that his reaction was angrier than it would otherwise have been because he was uncomfortable that, in the face of his brothers, he had not known where one of his daughters was, after dark. Majid chose this moment to make a complaint against Jasmine. Earlier in the day, she had answered her mother's mobile and, thinking that she was being clever by pretending to be an actress in a Turkish soap opera, she answered in a sing-song voice. Unfortunately, the caller was Majid. Her father was already raw and this was the last straw. He ordered her to the bathroom, followed her there and beat her.

His other brother, Nasser, and his friend called out "That's enough." We all sat like statues with our eyes down while this drama unfolded. Her father returned to the room and normal conversation was resumed. She went into one of the bedrooms to collect herself.

After ten minutes or so, she was sufficiently recovered to return to the room. No sooner had she done so, feeling relief that the trial was over, than Majid told her to go to the kitchen. He had a further complaint against her that he was going to deal with himself. She started to quake and was almost hyperventilating as he led her out to the kitchen. Her cries of terror were easily heard as he held her and shouted into her face. I could remain silent no longer.

"He is not her father. She has had enough." No one moved. I rose and said,

"I am going." I entered the kitchen, placed myself between them, put my hand on the arm that Majid was holding and said,

"Bass. Enough." Majid immediately dropped her arm and returned to the others. I told her to go to the safety of her bedroom. I returned to the room and made no attempt to hide my anger. I stayed a further ten minutes, without speaking, to ensure that there was no further complaint against Jasmine, and left.

In the winter of the following year, I helped Bassam's mother, H'layla, by twice driving her to the Queen Rania hospital, some thirty minutes' drive away. One of her knees was very painful. It was X-rayed on the first visit and she was asked to return two days later to see the orthopaedic surgeon. To thank me for taking her, she invited me to supper later that evening. I was surprised, but pleased, when Fatma told me that their family had also been invited.

At sunset, after the evening prayer, we walked up to H'layla's house. There was a small group already gathered around a calor gas heater. On our arrival, one of the men decided it was time for the men to move into an inner room, away from the women, while the women gathered together near the kitchen door. I was invited to sit on a cushion in the entrance hall, near the door to the men's room and from where I could see all the comings and goings.

Ahmad, Bassam's 11 year old son arrived with his pride and joy – a box radio playing Arab music. He stood nearby listening, with the radio close to his ear. At that moment Majid appeared and said something to him. I couldn't hear what was said but Ahmad immediately switched the radio off and put it down on top of the heater. Majid called out to his brother,

"Bassam, could I have a word with you please?" Bassam appeared from the inner room. I heard the words "radio" and "Chofa," Bassam's 15 year old daughter. Whatever was said, it was enough to cause Bassam to head for the kitchen angrily calling after Chofa. The women clustered around her, to prevent her father getting at her. Majid joined the melee. Chofa managed to escape and left the house, sobbing. The sound of shouting and recrimination reached fever pitch. I felt that to remain would be to condone what was happening, so I rose, put my shoes on and left.

Despite the uproar, my leaving the house was noticed and H'layla came after me calling "*Ta'alee. Ta'alee.* Come back. Come back." I stopped, trying to decide what to do. I saw Bassam and the rest of his family getting into their car. His mother then diverted her attention to them and repeated the same plea. "*Ta'al, ta'al.*" For H'layla's sake, I returned to the house, as did they.

I returned to my seat on the cushion and the men and women returned to their territories. Only Majid remained in the area of the kitchen and his mother indicated that he should seat himself by the heater and be quiet. He had his back to the same wall as me, but on the other side of the doorway to the men's room. I was two metres away from him but the stench of *arak* on his breath was quite clear. Peace reigned for five minutes and then he started again.

"Fatma – come here." So she, accompanied by H'layla for support, left the women's group by the kitchen and approached Majid. He started to make a complaint about the fact that Chofa had been seen in a shop buying a memory stick. He addressed her as if she were a naughty girl. She tried to explain that the teacher had asked the girls to provide themselves with memory sticks, so that they could save work that they had done on the school computer. He wasn't interested. As far as he was concerned, computers were no-go areas for women. Fatma submitted to his complaints whilst, at the same time, trying to move away from him. By now it was clear that he had been drinking very heavily. His face was dull and expressionless and his words were slurred.

Fatma returned to the kitchen. Majid then started to complain to his mother about his married sister whose husband, like Fatma's, was present in the inner room. It had been Majid who had stopped this sister from finishing her schooling. She was clever and had been one of only a few girls who had gone to school in Wadi Musa for post-16 education. Majid had heard that some youths from Wadi Musa had shouted at the girls through the bus window. That was enough for him. No more school. Within a few months, she was married and, within a year, a mother. He was the self-appointed judge of everyone else's behaviour, despite his being insensible with drink. Yet, no-one intervened. The women's husbands knew what he was doing. The women obeyed his summonses. His authority, by virtue of being male and a family member, was absolute.

I felt sickened at the way that this man was holding court. Once again I arose, put on my shoes and left, saying,

"I am not staying to listen to any more of this." Again, H'layla was told and came after me. This time, however, I had disappeared down a dark alley and she couldn't see me.

When the family returned home later, they brought my portion of the supper.

There can be very few societies in the world where over-indulgence in alcohol is *not* a problem. In addition, human frailty should be met with compassion. Yet, what I found so disturbing about this man's behaviour was, first, that his targets were always women and second, that the other men permitted his bad behaviour.

These incidents were also important because they prompted a shift in my approach to my neighbours. I had hoped that by showing kindness to and respect for the animals, the people around me might be encouraged to consider a different way of thinking themselves. In addition, I was very conscious that I was an interloper in this community. I had therefore tried very hard to honour and respect the behaviour of the people around me. Most had been born in tombs and caves. Like many in the Arab world, they knew nothing of the Renaissance or The Enlightenment or the Industrial Revolution or the female emancipation that resulted from the world wars. Literature, fine art and music were completely outside their experience.

The clashes with Majid showed me that I could not, and indeed that I *should* not stand idly by. I could not be just an observer. Maybe, in some small way, I could champion the women when they were powerless to help themselves.

Chapter 14
Ibrahim's Story

There were, however, at least two women in the village who did *not* need anyone's help with their man. These ladies were the two wives of Ibrahim of the Jamada tribe; Miriam and Hay'at.

I first met Ibrahim when out on a ride with Bassam. We were heading for Wadi Sabra, a southern suburb and entrance to the ancient city and important enough to have its own amphitheatre hewn from the bedrock which is still visible today. We needed to leave Petra city centre on a stony track which took us past the Great Temple. This is one of the largest buildings in Petra. Its superstructure had been badly damaged over the years by successive earthquakes but it had been lovingly excavated over a period of years by a team from Brown University, Rhode Island, USA. This particular day, a group of local men were working on cleaning and sorting the scattered building blocks.

Bassam called a greeting to one of them. He stopped his work and walked across to the track we were on. He was in his sixties, wiry, a little stooped and wearing the traditional red and white kefir headdress. He shook my hand warmly and smiled directly and unashamedly into my eyes. The wisdom of the ages was in his eyes. I instantly thought "What a lovely man!" Over the two years that I was working in Amman and visiting Petra at the weekend, I saw Ibrahim several times. He always recognised me, he always stopped what he was doing and he always exchanged some words with me. The better my Arabic became, the longer the exchange of words could be.

Not long after I had started living in Um Sayhoun, I was driving up the main street on my way to Wadi Musa when I saw Ibrahim standing on the side of the road, holding the hand of his five year-old son. By them, on the pavement, were two large jerry cans. I stopped and offered him a lift. He put the cans in the boot, and then sat in the front next to me with his son on his lap. As we went along, he explained that he had run out of benzene. Ibrahim had a little side business, selling benzene to his neighbours. There was no petrol station in Um Sayhoun and the nearest in Wadi Musa was well out of the town and high up on the wadi side. Not only was his stock of benzene exhausted but the petrol tank in his own pick-up was also empty. [This inability to forecast future events or consequences was very common in Jordan. It was particularly noticeable on the desert highway. Many male drivers simply could not bear to have a woman driver in front of them. She must be overtaken at all costs. So, if I was using the outside lane to overtake a lorry, many a time a male driver would roar up my nearside, trying to undertake, only to slam on the brakes to avoid driving into the back of the same lorry.]

I drove them up to the petrol station, where I was well known to the cigarette-smoking Egyptian petrol pump attendants. I waited while the purchase was made and the two full cans were replaced in the boot. Ibrahim then wanted me to drop him, his son and the jerry cans in the *souq* because he had other business to attend to. He was adamant that all would now be well and that he would find another lift home when he was ready. I went on to the Crowne Plaza where I sat in the sun, drank coffee and read the Jordan Times.

I next saw Ibrahim two weeks later. This time I was traditionally dressed and on foot down in Petra. I was probably on my way to Thraya's cave. I was crossing the bridge over the wadi where the donkey and camel men gather. I heard someone calling me.

"*Ta'alee Joanna. Ta'alee.* Come here, Joanna. Come here." It was Ibrahim. We smiled and greeted each other. He explained that the work for Brown University had finished for the season. As we spoke, he pulled a grubby handkerchief from his pocket and started unfolding it to reveal the contents. Ah. Disappointingly, he seemed to be on the point of trying to sell me Nabattean and Roman coins –a favourite occupation. Such treasures were fairly plentiful, if you knew where to look. New caches were often found after heavy rain when torrential rain cuts away the detritus of millennia and reveals the earth's hidden secrets.

This day, though, I became aware that he wasn't trying to sell me any coins. He wanted me to choose one as a gift for helping him with the benzene at our last meeting. This was awful. I really didn't want one of his coins and yet I couldn't deny him the means of showing his appreciation. Then my eye lighted on a black ring. It was paper-thin and seemed to have a carving of the Treasury on its flat, oval face. In one or two spots, there were vestiges of silver visible. I asked if I could have the ring instead of a coin. He was so pleased that I had found something that I wanted and immediately gave me the ring. It fitted my finger perfectly. We parted, both content.

Some months later, on a visit to England, I put the ring in silver-cleaning solution. My heart was pounding as the bubbles started to rise. I followed the instructions and lifted it after the appointed time. I started to rub it and, gradually, a beautiful shining silver ring emerged. I wear it to this day.

A couple of years after this, I was once again in the Crowne Plaza lobby. It was a cold winter's day and some of the local tour guides were taking shelter in the warmth of the hotel lobby, whilst awaiting their turn. I smiled across at them and settled to my newspaper. A little later, some of them moved off leaving just two, sitting together. I knew both of them by sight. One was in his thirties, open-faced and energetic. The other was older and wore the traditional headdress. I said,

"It is quiet for you today."

"Yes," they said, "it is." Suddenly, the elder said,

"I sold you alabaster two thousand years ago." I was speechless but I held his gaze. The younger man, embarrassed by his colleague's outburst said,

"Ah...he is just joking."

"No," I said. "I don't think that he is. I too believe in reincarnation." At that point, they were called to go and work. As they passed me on their way out, something made me relate the story of the ring. The elder man smiled and said,

"Ah. So you got your ring back then?" Thereafter, a knowing look always passed between us if we met at Petra or on the streets of Wadi Musa. I later learned that he was a well-respected sheikh at the biggest mosque in the town. I never asked, but I do believe that he tended towards Sufism, a very interesting, mystical branch of Islam.

The first time that I drank tea at Ibrahim's house, I realised that I already knew his first wife, Miriam. She was often to be seen at her jewellery stall in Petra, always welcoming, with a lovely smile on her face. She had four children, all in their twenties; three sons and a married daughter. Her two married sons had houses built on additional floors above her house. As Ibrahim saw me back to my car on that first visit, his daughters-in-law, not knowing that I understood them, shouted down from their balconies,

"Ha, Ibrahim, are you going to take another wife?" It was the start of a most wonderful friendship. I passed many hours in Ibrahim's yard. It was hard-baked earth with one mature olive tree. There had been two but only the trunk remained of the other. A public pathway ran along one side of the yard. Children often gathered on the low wall when word spread that I was there, but Ibrahim shoo'd them away.

There was a five year age gap between Miriam's youngest child and Hay'at's oldest. I never asked, of course, but I imagine that something must have happened to bring Miriam's child-bearing years to an end. So, after four or so years without a baby, Ibrahim had taken another wife, Hay'at. Her oldest daughter was sixteen. I do not know how many children she had but there must have been a new baby, on average, every 18 months, judging by the shapes and sizes of the children gathered around her. When I first met her, she was toothless. A year later, Ibrahim must have saved enough money for expensive dental treatment because Hay'at had a new set of teeth. I am no expert but they looked to me like implants rather than dentures. She had acquired new confidence and self-esteem which was lovely to see.

Ibrahim's family lived very simply on the ground floor. There was one communal room with a television and an adjacent kitchen. Off that room too, were two bedroom doors; one for each of his wives, I imagine. There was another door off the yard. This was occupied by Ibrahim's unmarried son, Haroun. There was the longest washing line I have ever seen. Wash day, which was almost every day, resembled my idea of a Chinese laundry.

I never, at any time, saw any wrong word pass between these ladies. As well as holding the fort at home with the children, Hay'at made dolls dressed as Bedouin women, for Miriam to sell at her stall in Petra. All the children were among the best behaved of my acquaintance. If Miriam and Hay'at were busy or tired, Ibrahim himself would make and serve the tea. I saw no other man do this. His family occasionally hosted feasts after Friday prayers. I was always invited.

Ibrahim was a regular worshipper at the only village mosque which stood opposite his house. He, of *all* the men in Um Sayhoun, was not embarrassed or uneasy at being seen talking to me on the street or, on occasion, if we met in the *souq* in Wadi Musa. If he saw my car on the street, he waved me down to ask how I was and to invite me to drink tea. He lingered over the handshake and sometimes continued to hold my hand as we talked – all without self-consciousness. He was a complete breath of fresh air. He lived a noble life without fear. There were so many things about his life which many westerners would find alien; a Moslem with two wives, living in a barren unyielding place and yet this lovely man had got it right. I admire him more than I can say. He truly is the salt of the earth.

Chapter 15
On Being Female

Baby girls are certainly welcomed into the world, especially if the family already has a male child. Unlike their older brothers, however, they are destined to leave their homes and their families. If a family has several daughters, at least one might remain with her parents in order to help with the domestic work. This isn't necessarily planned by the family but, if "no one comes", then this is the natural alternative role for the girl to fill. Interestingly, I was aware of at least two women who stayed at home until well into their thirties, and then married. They were never the first wife, however; always the second, or even the third.

Unlike their mothers and their grandmothers, girls these days go to school. It is a wonderful liberation for them – to be out of the house during school hours. Thraya's daughters would arrive for school every morning, having ridden in on their donkeys from their cave at *Hamdooda*, near the Snake Monument. They 'parked' their donkeys behind their father's house in clear view of my doorway. Their patient beasts would wait for them in the sun until the end of the school day and after family visits in the village had been made.

The girls enjoy their time at school and the school itself is well run and well ordered. Only one of the ten or so teachers was from Um Sayhoun. Most were from the neighbouring town of Wadi Musa. The cleaners and tea-makers were, however, village women. I used to visit the school occasionally. There, as everywhere else, it was assumed that I was well-off and could afford charity, although I made it very clear that I was living on a pension. On more than one occasion, the Headmistress asked me if I could provide some lined exercise books and pencils for the girls whose families sent them to school without the required resources. For less than £5 at the bookshop in Wadi Musa, I could buy twenty books and the same number of pencils. When I returned to the school and handed them over, the teachers asked me where I had got them from and were stunned when I had told them that I had bought them with my own money. Once, on leaving the staffroom in the company of two of the teachers, they repeated their question in disbelief.

"We would never do that," they said. *"Allah ma'kee. God be with you."*

Although the girls valued their education, the same could not be said of their text books. Very often, if the children upstairs were fighting, one of their text books would come flying over the balcony, landing in my yard. It was sometimes there for several days before Fatma, usually, came to collect it.

Jordanian education is centralised. If it is 15th May, it must be page 32. The English text books were particularly disappointing. Very few pupils, unless they had help at home, were able to speak English as a result of following the national course. It seemed to me that exposure to the language was not properly graded. The text books for seven year olds had passages about tropical fish, complete with names that even I had never heard of.

The school uniform consisted of trousers, usually

decorated jeans, with a long-sleeved tunic that fell to just above the knee. After puberty the girls would wear white scarves around their heads with not a hair showing. With puberty also came an increase in domestic duties. By the age of thirteen or fourteen, most girls could cook the big family meal and they were responsible for the family's laundry. School attendance was not now so regular as their mothers required them to be at home. If the mother worked at Petra, the girls' absences from school would be frequent. She would stay at home to do the chores, look after her younger siblings and be ready to provide drinks and food should her father, brother or a male relative so require.

It was not unusual for fifteen-year-old girls in the top class to be engaged or even married while they were still at school. Very few girls stayed at school past sixteen. The top class usually had about twenty five girls in it. Of those, only two or three would continue with post-sixteen education in Wadi Musa. Bassam's oldest daughter Chofa, was one of

A baby is rocked by the wind

three in her year to do so. One of the girls dropped out in the first term. In the summer term of her first year, I noticed that Chofa was at home during the day. I asked her why and she explained that her father had stopped her going to school. One of the donkey men at Petra had reported to Bassam that he had seen Chofa walking through the *souq,* or market area in Wadi Musa. The *souq* lay between the Girls' School and the bus station. So, in order to travel home, Chofa had to walk that route. As far as the men of Um Sayhoun were concerned, Chofa was putting herself in a vulnerable position. One of the ways of referring to a daughter in Arabic is *il-ma'roosa,* the guarded one. Public spaces are male. So, for some men, any female on their territory was fair game for whistles and shouts. What's more, she was abroad in the land of the 'enemy' in Wadi Musa.

A couple of days after I had spoken to Chofa, I had the opportunity to ask Bassam about it. He said that she could return to school if he could find someone from the village to take her door-to-door at the beginning and end of the day. I do not know whether or not this was later arranged, but I was very pleased to see that Chofa had returned to school. It may or may not have been as a result of a question that I put to Bassam.

"Do you want your daughters and your sons' daughters to be taught, forever, by women from Wadi Musa?

Being of marriageable age, she was considered to be the most in need of protection by the male family members. Her every action was scrutinised. If she were going to either of her grandmothers houses, her eyes must be down, she must be on the street for the minimum time and she must not stop to talk to anyone, not even another woman. That would have been tantamount to putting herself on display.

One afternoon, Fatma and I were sitting quietly in my

entrance hall, drinking Bedouin tea. Suddenly, we heard Chofa approaching, shouting out in fear and clearly very frightened.

"Ahmed is after me! Ahmed is after me." Ahmed is her well-educated, oldest, bachelor uncle.

"Go into the inner room," I said. "Shut the door and stay there."

Almost immediately, her drunken uncle staggered through the door. Fatma tried to stop him coming in, but he raised his arm and struck her on the jaw with his forearm, sending her reeling back, stunned, her *hejab* disarranged. Next he made for the closed door, kicking the tea tray and scattering its contents as he did so. I lifted the white, plastic, stacking chair that I was sitting on and tried to restrain him by pushing its legs against him. He looked momentarily stunned.

"I will call the police," I cried.

"Fuck you and fuck the police," was his retort.

At that moment, Chofa emerged from her hiding place. In her trembling hand was a serrated-edged kitchen knife with a six inch blade. With great resolve and courage, she stood and faced him, uttering a stream of words in the Bedouin dialect that I was hard-pressed to understand. Whatever she had said stopped him in his tracks. The stand-off lasted half a minute more before a younger male cousin arrived, smilingly try to calm Ahmed, and eventually led him away.

We felt relief but we also felt anger. Her 'crime' had been that she had been up on the flat roof of the house, properly dressed in every way, in order – at her mother's request – to check the water levels in the three tanks. He regarded it as a flagrant attempt to display herself.

It is an unspoken assumption that every girl, unless she is in some way disfigured or disabled, will marry young and will start a family quickly. Among my neighbours, there were two young women who had been allowed to break the mould. One was a policewoman and the other was in the army; both working away from their own district. I thought that they looked splendid in their uniform, complete with white *hejabs* under their berets, as they walked to the bus to return to their unit each week. It made me so happy to see these women successfully pursuing a life outside the village and away from their men folk. What a good example to others, I thought; until I was told that they could never marry anyone from the village because their fathers could not guarantee a groom's requirement that his bride should be a virgin.

Marriages usually take place in the summer months. The celebrations last three days and culminate in the groom and his family arriving to collect the bride from her home and to take her to her new home, where she hopes that her mother-in-law will be kind. These days, she is beautifully dressed in a western-style bridal gown. The morning will have been spent at the salon, having her hair coiffed and her make-up done. As she awaits her new husband, she is seated on a raised throne in a room for women only. The groom enters and is allowed to see her but, before she can be taken out to public view, a white, hooded, monk-like cape is placed over her, so that no other male has sight of her hair or her uncovered neckline. A car and driver will have been hired to take her to her new home where she is taken to another women-only room, her cape removed and she is re-seated on another raised throne.

The female guests bring her gifts of money, quite often just a small amount or whatever can be afforded. There is usually very loud amplified music and the girls in new dresses, and the young boys in miniature suits mill around in great excitement. Quite often, during this process, one of the mature women steps up onto the throne, places her mouth right next to the bride's ear and proceeds to pass on whatever delicate information that she thinks will help the bride both on her wedding night and in times to come. I used to feel such compassion for these young brides. They were fulfilling their own dreams and their families' expectations but, for most of them, this was the start of a life spent in the home, bearing children, feeding their families, meeting their husband's needs, probably tending the family goats and, later, helping to care for their husbands' parents. It would be a long time before they achieved the status of matriarch and, with it, a certain independence of action.

Usually, within a year, the first child is born. Delayed pregnancies are often the source of interesting gossip. These days, most women deliver their children in the local hospital. In times past, in the tombs and caves, the women simply helped each other. Everyone born in those days can tell you which woman was attending their mother at the birth. Following the birth of the first child, the new mother moves to her mother-in-law's house where a room is set aside for her and her visitors. She stays there for forty days, sleeping alone, being cared for by the women of the family. I began to notice a gradual change in this custom. More often now, the new mother remains at home, attended by her sisters, but still sleeping alone for the traditional forty days.

Thereafter she does what all women do. She tries to fulfil the community's expectations of a good woman. If her husband brings non-family male guests to the house, she will cook her finest *mansaf,* but she will not appear before them, even though she is properly dressed with her head covered. She stands outside the men's room, holding the large platter and calling to her husband to come and collect the food. She is totally dependent on her husband for money. Sometimes a husband will ask why his evening meal is meagre or without meat. She has to explain that she had nothing in the house and had to borrow the necessary ingredients from a neighbour. If a new gas cylinder were needed for cooking, the husband would leave the money before going down to Petra.

Hard as the work was, and long the day, women whose husbands' permitted, enjoyed working in Petra because it gave them a little money in their own purses. These purses were precious and were suspended around their necks on long cords and tucked under the *fustan* or *madraga,* depending on the woman's choice of clothing. Latterly, these purses contained old model mobile phones. These were generally considered to be dangerous items for a woman to possess and the men were slow to provide them. However, the men quickly saw the advantage of being able to summon their wives from tending the goats or drinking tea in neighbours' houses, when their plans changed, or if they were returning with tourists and wanted to offer them Bedouin tea. The incoming and outgoing call records were routinely checked by the men. Being illiterate and unable to read the phone screen, the women aged thirty and above had to memorise the pattern of characters in numbers that were safe to answer. They didn't make calls. The phones were simply to facilitate their availability.

Like members of a trade union in the West, the greatest weapon a woman had in her dealings with her husband, was withdrawal of services. If a woman felt hard-done-by or if she had had a serious row with her husband or if he had been drinking or if it had been reported to her that he was seen talking to another woman on the street, she would take her youngest child and return to her father's house. If her father were dead, she would go to her mother's or to her brother's. She would wait there until her husband indicated that he wanted her back. This state of affairs usually lasted two or three days; unusually it could last as long as a week. Sometimes, the husband himself would go to collect her. At other times, his best friends would go on his behalf. It was very rare for a woman to decline the invitation to return. Indeed, she glowed with pride if two, three or even four of her husband's friends had been sent to fetch her.

A neighbour called Hoodah must have thought that she had made a success of her thirty-year marriage. She had given her husband sons and daughters. She and her husband had borne together the loss of one of their sons in the incident with the police which had also killed Bassam's brother Abdullah. She had kept his house and his animals to the best of her ability, but it wasn't enough.

I had first met her on the mountains. She and her husband were working together to clear some of the stones from a patch of land in preparation for planting wheat. Less than a year later, her husband took a young, second wife and set up home with her away from the village in a traditional Bedouin tent. He signed his house over to his oldest son who, against the advice of everyone, sold it to a man from another family group. The son, who was living with his family in a rented house, used the money to buy a hundred sheep. The new owner allowed Hoodah and her unmarried daughters to stay in the house for one year, paying rent.

After that the three women had to move to a one-room unit right on the street with no land. Hoodah fed herself and her daughters by working at the portable public toilets near the entrance to Petra. She worked from 6 am to 6 pm, seven days a week. Her place of work was an hour's walk from her home.

Every house in the village had a television set. The women and girls spent quite a lot of time each day watching the various channels provided by Nilesat. A favourite was a Turkish soap opera called Nour, dubbed into Arabic. They watched, fascinated, the lives of these women from a secular Islamic country; heads uncovered, jobs, boyfriends, driving cars and living in palatial homes. It was another world. A world that would never be theirs.

One channel showed heavily-censored Hollywood films with Arabic sub-titles. I remember once watching a film with which I was sufficiently familiar to allow me to spot the censor's cuts. I was particularly incensed when I realised that a chaste kiss on the cheek had been cut but a scene in which a husband grabs the hair at the back of his wife's neck and proceeds to beat her head against the door upright, was left in, untouched.

I have written that two of the ways in which the society tried to control the men were fear of authority on the one hand and, on the other, the expectation that they would live within the Islamic code as interpreted by their Imams. The men themselves were responsible for trying to follow the Five Pillars of Islam; the profession of their faith, praying five times a day, helping the poor, fasting during Ramadan and the *hajj,* making the pilgrimage to Mecca. However, an important part of the dogma concerns guidance on the relationship between men and women. It gradually became clear to me that much of the responsibility for the latter was placed squarely on the shoulders of the women. Fortunately, according to the received wisdom, women have a very low libido and do not therefore suffer from problematic thoughts. Many of the men, however, believe that if they have an impure or lustful thought, they will go to hell: hence, in part, the dress of the women. Rather like the notion in Victorian society in the United Kingdom,

when heavy cloths were draped over furniture to conceal
the lower legs of tables and pianos, a woman must never
show her ankles. Ideally, her feet will be covered with thick
socks. The supra-sternal notch at the base of the neck must
never be visible, neither must her forearms. My neighbour
Fatma was doing some hand-washing at her home one day
when her youngest son, then aged five, entered the kitchen
and saw that she had pushed her sleeves above her elbows
to stop them getting wet.

"You are dirty," he said, meaning that her behaviour
was immodest.

The hair is of major concern. The rules concerning who
may have sight of a women's hair are strictly laid down.
Her husband, of course, has the right, as do her brothers.
Her brothers-in-law, however, do not. All the girls and
women wear their hair long, in order to be the more
beautiful when uncovered. The hair must therefore be tied
back in order to fit neatly under the *hejab*. The girls are
taught in their Religious Instruction lessons at school, that
the hair must be gathered low into the nape of the neck, and
not taken high onto their heads, rather in the style of the
beautiful Queen Nefertiti of ancient Egypt. No attention
must be drawn to it.

On the occasions when I was invited to eat at a
neighbour's house, I always wore traditional dress.
However, I always left a small portion of hair visible at the
front – an area of maybe two inches by half an inch. This
was too much for the older women. Even before words of
greeting had been uttered, they put their hands to their
heads to indicate to me that I was improperly dressed.

If I were going to visit a hotel in Wadi Musa in order to
catch up with the newspapers, I usually wore western
clothes, albeit modestly. I did this for two reasons; first, for
the greater comfort and weight of fabric and second,

because I wanted to demonstrate to the men that I was the same good woman, whatever I was wearing. On one occasion I had done some errands for one of Fatma's sisters and called at her house on my way home. I had not been in her house two minutes before she said,

"Why are you appearing before my husband with your head uncovered?"

I have said that one of the expressions for a daughter or young woman is *il-ma'roosa,* she who must be protected. Who, I ask, is she to be protected from? It seems illogical, to identify a potential threat to a young woman *and*, at the same time, to make that same potential victim entirely responsible for deterring that threat or, even, the idea of that threat.

In addition to the Koran itself, there are a series of writings called the *Hadith.* These were written by the men closest to Prophet Mohammed. They are reports, with varying degrees of accuracy, of what the Prophet had said on different subjects. These writings include:

Narrated 'Imran bin Husain: The Prophet said, *"I looked at Paradise and found poor people forming the majority of its inhabitants; and I looked at Hell and saw that the majority of its inhabitants were women."* Hadith – Sahih Bukhari 4:464.

I had tried to protect the animals. Now I felt that I needed to turn my attention to the women. Could I help the women to feel better about their bodies? Could I help the men to understand that women are a lot more than their bodies? It was going to be a delicate business.

Chapter 16
Amani's Story

Amani is a neighbour. She is twenty nine years old but she looks forty five. Her eyes are extremely beautiful but her cheeks are sunken. I have known her for six years. I say 'known' but what I mean is 'communicated.' For several years, my Arabic was not good enough to visit my neighbours, except to smile at their children and to show by my facial expression and my body language, that I was comfortable with them and that I honoured and valued their lives.

In recent years, with the improvement in my Arabic, that changed. I could now pay visits and engage in conversation. From the beginning, Amani had always made her eyes available to me as I was passing, either on foot or in my car. There was always a warm smile and a wave from her. At one time, another neighbour was away, making a pilgrimage to Mecca, leaving her eight children to the care of her husband and the neighbours. I, like other women, took food from time to time to help feed the family in her absence. Amani was always there, ready to see that the children shared fairly or, if necessary, to put the food in the fridge.

One day, I saw Amani coming out of the free clinic. She looked sad and, unusually, her face showed signs of despair.

"*Shoo mushkilah*? What is the problem?" I asked. The doctor had told her,

"You are starving. You need dried milk. Get yourself some fruit juice." What a joke. A packet of dried milk costs four Jordanian dinars, about £3.50, and a carton of fruit juice, half that amount. Amani has four children all under eight. Four years ago, her husband took a second wife, with whom he now has two children. He divided his house in two.

Amani and her four children live in one room, thinly carpeted with foam mattresses around three walls. There is no light bulb and the room opens directly onto a dirty street. To go to their rudimentary toilet and kitchen, Amani and her children have to go out onto the street and along to another door. Her two oldest children are girls of eight and six. They have never been to school because there is no money for the shapeless tunics the girls are required to wear. The next child, a five year-old boy who needed no special clothes, started school last year with the other boys.

Amani's husband has one donkey. Some days he goes to Petra to try to earn money from the tourists. On other days, he smokes *heeshee*, a form of pot. He follows the Koran in treating his two wives equally when it comes to night-time visiting. I am not sure that there is similarly equal treatment when it comes to the distribution of his meagre income.

That day, at the clinic, it had been confirmed that she was expecting her fifth child. I bought the dried milk and the fruit juice. On my visits to the *souq al hudra*, the vegetable market, I bought extra bananas and other seasonal fruit. As and when I could, I gave her small amounts of money, maybe two to three dinars each time. Her children were thrilled and excited whenever I visited.

"Sit down," they would say. "Drink tea with us." They were well and happy. Their mother was starving.

The realisation was dawning that I should actively try to subvert the men's attitude to the women. This coincided with my having acquired enough Arabic – and sufficient familiarity with the Bedouin dialect – both to understand more of what was going on around me and to assert myself as and when the need arose.

This, then, was the social melting pot that was my home for so many years. In such a climate, what did they make of me? How did I win their trust? How, indeed, did I survive? A series of challenging situations were to force me out into the open; no longer could I play the part of the docile, accepting guest in their midst. Humility can look like weakness and arrogance like strength. The time had come to redress the balance.

Chapter 17
Having to Resist

At risk of stating the obvious, when I first arrived in the Bedouin village, my neighbours simply did not know what to make of me. They could understand my love of the mountains but what was less easy for them to comprehend was that I should want to live alone in the village. Why didn't I marry someone from the village? It would be much better if I did. Indeed, many of them assumed until the very day that I left, despite the thirty-year age difference, Bassam and I were lovers. Why else would I be there?

Despite their puzzlement, when it was seen that I was a good woman and that I didn't have gentlemen callers, they were quick to accept me and to invite me to their homes. For most of them, these were acts of outright kindness. For some, the apparent kindness provided an opportunity to ask for favours or to judge what use I could be to them. This was a constant problem. It was important that I should treat my friends and neighbours in Um Sayhoun and Wadi Musa with politeness and respect, but I was always wary, waiting for the favour to be asked. Could I drive the family to Aqaba to visit the doctor? Could I lend them money? Could I teach their children English at no cost? Why didn't I sit in the front seat of the taxi, next to the driver? Why did I insist on travelling in the back?

The politeness and courtesy could never be switched off. Good, plausible reasons had to be found as to why I couldn't accede to their requests. To achieve that, I admit that I often had to bend the truth. I became a master of resistance.

The resistance had to be on two fronts. The first was resisting my neighbours. The other was trying to fight elements of the very culture. My ability to assert myself when I needed to was aided by the fact that I had first earned their respect. This had taken some years and had cost me dear. It had been achieved in several ways.

For many years, on Saturdays when there was no school and Bassam was busy working at Petra, I would drive Fatma and the children down the mountain road where we would pick a spot to light a fire and cook *casteer,* the delicious lunch made on the fire with the food in an aluminium foil parcel. This particular day, we had chosen a lovely spot with plenty of wood for the fire and shade to sit under. The food was nearly ready and beginning to smell delicious when Jasmine suddenly called out,

"*Dooda, dooda.*" Fatma was instantly alert and clearly frightened. I had no idea what *dooda* was.

"*Wain?* Where?" she called. Jasmine pointed. We followed her finger and there, side-winding through the undergrowth and making for our food was a heavy-looking snake about two metres long. The children ran away, trusting Fatma and me to do something. Fatma had a long stick in her hand that she had been using to control the fire. She moved quickly and, with amazing accuracy, hit the snake on the head. It was stunned. The blow had stopped its forward momentum but its tail was still waving lazily. Fatma stood holding the head down with the stick. With my heart pounding and my eyes scanning the ground for anything that I could use to help her, I picked up a stone the size of a honeydew melon. The first drop had to count but I was wary of getting close enough to ensure that I was accurate. I nevertheless stepped forward and dropped the stone directly onto the snake's head. I killed it.

The children crept back, but Fatma made them stay away. She used her long stick to pick up the snake and to hang it over a branch some metres from the fire. I took a photograph of it with my mobile phone. We ate our lunch, packed and went, never to return to that spot. Back home, our exploit soon became the talk of the village. People flocked to see the photograph. It was judged to be a deadly snake. If it had bitten any of us, that person would have died in the time that it would have taken to reach the

The dead snake.

hospital. Later, one of the men said to me, in broken but very eloquent English,

"That snake...it loves no-one."

A couple of years after that incident, my worst mistake also provided my neighbours with further means of trying to measure me. In an act of extreme arrogance, I bought a mule. Or rather, Bassam bought it on my behalf. She was big and black and I kept her in my yard not four metres from the door. A saddle was bought and I made a soft, padded saddle blanket. Bassam helped me buy wheat and *berseem*, the dried alfafa used for animal feed. I called her Zeeza.

We had some excellent rides together, including visits to Saloom's tent and to Wadi N'meera with its Greek inscription. These were our happiest times, despite the fact that she walked slowly and nothing that I could do would chivvy her up. Everyone greeted me with pleasure as I rode her. Some of the men said,

"Ah...I know that mule. She's the one who likes to walk slowly." Indeed she did. It was foolish of me, to think that I could mount her and then expect her to obey my instructions as if I were driving a car. She gradually realised that she would always win the battle of wills, because I would not mistreat her. When the men realised that she was becoming unmanageable, they said,

"You've got to hit her. She's got to be afraid of you." The crunch came one day when I wanted to ride her to Petra. In order to mount her, I had to find a ledge or large rock. As we were approaching my usual mounting block, she thought,

"I don't like the look of this and, anyway, it's very hot today." She pulled the reins out of my hand, turned on her hooves and went back up the hill.

"Right," I thought. You are not going to spoil my plans

for the day and I carried on, on foot. When I returned home later in the day, there she was in her tethering place, saddle still in place and waiting for me to feed her. The next day, I let it be known that I wanted to sell her. I had bought her for seven hundred Jordanian dinars. I said I wanted six hundred. Nobody came, although several, seeing an opportunity for a cut, offered to arrange a sale for me. Weeks went by and the animal wasn't being properly exercised. I eventually sold her for two hundred dinars to one of Fatma's brothers who declared her to be almost as fast as a race horse!

My failure served, in some way, to enhance the skills of my neighbours. Ah, they thought, she tried to copy our skills but she can't handle animals like we can. Indeed, I couldn't and I wouldn't.

Another incident which helped me gain not only acceptance, but also the respect of my neighbours, arose from a tragedy. One morning in February 2010, news quickly spread through the village that Awad, the eight-year-old son of Hunnan and her husband, another Bassam, had died. He had been down in the wadi with his mother, tending the goats. The lack of rainfall in the preceding months had been desperate and one of the wealthier families had decided to hire a mechanical digger, to try to find water. The attempt had failed. However, apparently mercifully, there had been some heavy rain and the hole had filled with water. It had been a while since Awad and his mother had come to this spot with their goats and Awad was delighted to see the pool of water. He had been playing on the steep banks of the artificially created hole and had fallen in. No Bedouin child and, to my knowledge, no Bedouin man can swim. There are no public swimming baths and the hotel pools in neighbouring Wadi Musa are not for them.

Awad struggled and his mother's cries attracted the notice of other women nearby. She undid the shawl from her head and tried to throw an end to him. When she failed, the women had to stop her entering the water herself to save him. A passing man called for help on his mobile but it did not come soon enough. The desperate mother watched as her son lost his battle to stay afloat. She watched as his body sank from sight. She watched as it reappeared on the surface and she watched as it finally sank.

A four-by-four appeared. A man tied one end of a long rope around the back of the vehicle and the other around his waist. He held his breath and disappeared from sight. Half a minute later he reappeared, carrying the boy's body. Everyone was stunned at such a tragedy.

The following day, I donned traditional clothes and went to the *azer,* the three days of mourning when the bereaved receive visits of condolence. A tent was pitched for the men's *azer* and the women held theirs in the inner rooms. I arrived and sat in an outer room, not wanting to intrude on the inner room where Hunnan and her sisters and friends were gathered. However, news of my arrival spread and Hunnan sent word that I was to go to her. The grief in her room was palpable. I approached her, shook her hand and kissed her cheek, struggling to utter the words of condolence.

"Uth'm Allah ajrakum." She seated me close to her. Dates and cardamom-flavoured coffee were served. She regained her composure and started to talk about Awad. He was a very clever boy. He was top in his year group at school. He rode in your car.

"What?" I asked.

"Yes. Last week he came home, excited. He was walking back from Beda. You stopped and gave him a lift. He said you were very kind." I remembered. He had told me his name, but I had no idea that it was the same boy. Such a simple act of kindness on my part was being acknowledged with honour by this grief-stricken mother.

The final incident which demonstrates, in part, how I had achieved a position from which I could say difficult things to my neighbours happened like this. A wedding was being celebrated at my neighbour's house. It was the final day of the festivities when the bride was to be brought from her father's home. I had drunk tea with the women for a while and then returned home to put on my best *fustan* and shawl, ready to join the procession.

I became aware of the sound of a goat bleating. It was a desperate sound. I looked out of the window and saw, up on the road, an adult goat being held by a boy. Surely they haven't left it this late to slaughter a goat for the festivities, was the thought that crossed my mind. I went out and called to the boy,

"Is there a problem?"

"This goat has cut herself on some corrugated iron. It is one of Bassam's. He has sent for the animal doctor and he is coming." Relieved at this news, I re-entered the house and completed my preparations. The agonising bleating continued. Finally I was ready to rejoin the other women. As I climbed the steps up onto the road, I looked to my right and saw on Bassam's terrace that he, the vet and the boy were bending over the nanny goat. Despite my Bedouin finery, something made me join them. I heard the boy whisper to the men,

"Joanna jai. Joanna is coming." Their eyes flicked up as they continued their work. The goat's legs had been tied. Bassam was holding her back legs apart so that the vet could access the injuries. The boy was pinning her down by her neck. Her injuries were awful. Her abdomen and udder were lacerated and the vet was busy stitching the wound,

his surgical gloves covered with blood. I knew this man. He had had to attend my mule when she had had a problem with her leg. He had quietly admired by the way in which I had held onto her ear to keep her still while he injected her.

The men ignored me. No word was spoken. I squatted by the goat's head. I stroked it gently and started to talk to her.

"I know you are in distress but you will feel better when they have finished. It won't be long now. He has nearly finished." She immediately fell silent, as if listening to me. In my peripheral vision, I saw the men's heads snap up to exchange a quick glance. The goat remained silent and I stayed by her. I could see that the stitching was complete and that a bottle of iodine was being unscrewed.

"This might sting," I said. Whether or not it did, the goat didn't utter another sound. The job done and her bonds loosened, she was quickly on her feet, shaking away the indignity of it all. I walked away. Thirty minutes later, the girls and younger boys were fighting to hold my hands in the wedding procession.

I had tried to be a good neighbour. My kitchen almost became an additional store for the family upstairs. Did I have cumin, turmeric, onions, garlic, courgettes, lemons? The list was endless. This presented no problem. The family were generous in their invitations for me to eat with them. Help such as this was an easy way of returning their generosity.

The vacuum cleaner was another treasure that was often borrowed.

The girls who visited my house were fascinated by the European toilet. I used to let them use it when they asked. One day, a girl on the street admired the colour of my lipstick. Had I got any more? She wanted one.

"No. This is the only one I have." Two days later,

another girl visited and then asked to use the toilet. The next day, when I wanted to 'do my face', the lipstick was gone. The same thing happened a few weeks later, with a different girl. This time it was the only mascara I owned. Thereafter, when they asked to visit the loo, I would say,

"If you need to use a toilet, go home." After that there were fewer visits.

The greatest and most frequent help that I could give the women was in the use of my car. Once the menfolk had decided that I was acceptable, the women were quick to take advantage. On my trips to Wadi Musa, I always stopped for women waiting on the street. Often they needed to go to the doctor or the free clinic. Sometimes married women in twos would be going to the *souq* for food shopping. My car became known as the *taxi al niswaan*, the women's taxi. It was not a taxi in the sense that I charged them, because I didn't. Taxi was the word they gave to any saloon car or, indeed, any car which was not a pick-up.

Indeed, doctors and hospital visits were a grand opportunity for some rare freedom for the women. I even suspected some of creating a set of symptoms which needed attention, in order to have an excuse to travel. The diary entries in chapter 10 frequently feature such excursions.

Fatma's sister, Hadeeja, lived just down the road from me. Her husband did not have a car. She had seven children, among whom were two tearaway boys aged six and eight. About five or six times over a two year period, I was summoned, usually late in the evening, to take one or other of them to the hospital. On one occasion, the younger boy had been kicked by a donkey, probably deservedly, and needed stitches in his chin. I once asked Hadeeja,

"How do you get to the hospital when I am not here?"

"We call the *balance,*" she replied. "But they are not good. They don't always come."

I had been feeling unwell for some days. It had been unusually cold, with even daytime temperatures only reaching five or six degrees. In addition, a cold *Shmarli* wind had been blowing from Syria in the north, filling the air with sand and dust. For several nights, my sleep had been interrupted by the rattling sounds issuing from my chest. In addition, on three successive preceding days, I had driven neighbours to the public hospital a half hour's drive away from the village. The 65 year old mother of fourteen children and a four week old baby girl had both been admitted with chest infections.

It was 7.20 in the evening and I was about to shut down my computer and enjoy some home-made vegetable soup while watching a film from my DVD collection. The doorbell rang. Five seconds later, as I was on my way to the door, it rang again.

"Anna jai. Anna jai. I'm coming. I'm coming," I shouted. It was Hadeeja. Her three year-old daughter, Yasmin, had been sick and was clearly unwell. Could I drive them to the hospital? Hadeeja's husband keeps his family by running a café at the High Place of Sacrifice in Petra. He uses donkeys to get himself and his stock from his home to the site. This involves a 220 metre descent to the Petra main street, followed by an ascent of 180 metres. He takes turns with two of his sons to sleep at the site. That night, it was his turn to be away from home.

Our journey to the hospital would take us past an excellent local doctor whose surgery would still be open. However, Hadeeja did not want to go there. She wanted to receive free treatment for her daughter, if she could, and that meant the hospital. So, armed with a black plastic bag against further sickness, Hadeeja and Yasmin climbed into my car. The hospital stands on a barren mountainside near the summit of a very high ridge; so high that snow can sometimes be seen there and nowhere else.

The A and E Department looked relatively quiet as we approached. Yasmin's name and age were taken and we were directed to a curtained booth. Hadeeja lifted the child onto the bed. Yasmin was happy to sit upright but not to lie back. Within four minutes a doctor arrived and Hadeeja told her story. The doctor left and returned with a spatula. In an unguarded moment, Yasmin allowed the spatula into her mouth but then bit down on it like a vice. She held it so tightly that the doctor could do nothing with it. Some coaxing eventually released the spatula. A cry of fright opened the child's mouth for a split second during which time the doctor was able to see the back of her throat and to diagnose a viral infection. The hospital pharmacy was closed for the night so the doctor offered a prescription to be taken to the duty pharmacist in the local town. Hadeeja was not happy, partly because she didn't want to pay but also, as it turned out, because the child would not take medicines orally. She wanted her child to have an injection at the hospital. The doctor disagreed.

Two minutes later a male nurse, a lovely man who knew me well from my many previous visits, arrived with an oral syringe of orange syrup. The child was having none of this. The nurse's one and only attempt to administer the antibiotic was met with a tightly sealed mouth, causing the syrup to trickle down her chin and onto her jacket. The syringe was pushed into my hand with the words, "You do it." I made a brave attempt and failed. Her mother knew better than to try. A kindly man from Um Sayhoun who was visiting someone in the next cubicle, appeared around the curtain and offered the child a chocolate. The child's eyes lit up and her hand stretched out for the sweet. I took it and promised that it would be hers the moment she had drunk the syrup. I had no sooner spoken than the girl's mother took the chocolate from me, unwrapped it and gave it to the child. Yasmin had no trouble in opening her mouth for that. My patience was all but spent.

We left the cubicle and Hadeeja stood at the counter, waiting for a prescription. I stood to one side, away from what was now a crush of potential patients. I felt so ill and exhausted that I leaned on the wall behind me. In my haste to help Hadeeja, I was modestly but not traditionally dressed. At that moment, a woman from Wadi Musa began to walk past me. She had a female relative in tow. She was smartly dressed, with a coloured *hejab*. She was fairly tall with a ram-rod straight back. Her thoughts were written all over her face. Who is this foreigner, daring to be different, invading our public facilities? With a smirk she passed unnecessarily close to me. The corridor was wide but she wanted to indicate that I was mistaken if I thought that the space I was temporarily occupying was mine. I knew that she would look back to see if her friend had been impressed by her gesture. I wasn't disappointed. Her head began to turn slowly. However, she was not expecting my eyes to be waiting for her. I held her gaze long enough to try to transmit my disappointment at her arrogance.

With the prescription safe in Hadeeja's hand, we began our journey back. I didn't know whether Hadeeja had enough money for the medicines, so I asked whether she wanted to go to the chemist or straight home. She wanted to go to the chemist. Mercifully, I was able to park directly outside. She took the child with her and went in. I stayed in the car and closed my eyes, exhausted by the evening's events. Two to three minutes later, I opened my eyes to find that she was no longer at the shop counter. I knew that the doctor's surgery was on the floor above the chemist. I dragged myself out of the car, locked it and climbed the four flights of stairs to the surgery. I asked a young man if he had seen a woman with a small child. The doctor heard my voice, opened the surgery door and invited me in.

I was just in time to see the nurse hand a syringe to the doctor. Hadeeja was holding Yasmin face-down on the doctor's couch, her little bottom exposed in preparation for the injection. The indignant cries of the child filled the surgery. Hadeeja was triumphant. On the way home in the car, Hadeeja said,

"What time is it? About 8 o'çlock?"

"No," I said, "It is 10 o'çlock."

"Ah," she said, "I think that we are all a bit tired."

Yes. Indeed.

I really wanted to be the means of giving these ladies a break from their homes and children. I wanted to see them act independently and even to go paddling in Aqaba if they wanted to, but the physical wear and tear on me was becoming too high a price to pay in order to give them a taste of what, to me, was normal life. So, I always tried to help with medical emergencies but, in later years, I stopped telling the ladies when I was planning a trip.

Another favourite destination was a Bangladeshi lady doctor in the potash-mining town of Al Hisa, an hour and a quarter's drive away. For a long time, I drove the ladies there, free of charge. Then I started to say,

"I will drive you there but I need some petrol money." Most women looked at me with disappointment and indignation and went home. One day, my neighbour Gasseem's wife, Airlia, wanted to visit this lady doctor. She asked how me how much it would be. Eight dinars, I said. This was the exact cost of the petrol. She went home and asked Gasseem, who told her that a taxi driver would charge her twenty dinars. We had a happy outing. At the petrol station, she gave me the money and then, after the consultation, she bought me a bottle of fruit juice and a cake by way of thanks.

Little by little, I felt that I was achieving some success in resisting the demands of my neighbours. Then, in March 2010, something happened which made me want to resist the very culture I was living in. The report of a terrible court case appeared in the Jordan Times, the English language daily. An Amman man had been sentenced to five years imprisonment and his sons, who were aged 14 and 17 at the time of the crime, to 1 and 2 years in juvenile detention. Their crime was that they had beaten a 19 year old woman to death. The woman was the man's daughter and the sister of the two boys.

The woman had told her father that she was going shopping at the local shops. Later, one of her uncles saw her on the street. The parade of shops was long and she had strayed into the neighbouring district. The uncle stopped his car and took her home. There, he reported his findings to her father. Incensed, the father tied his daughter to a tree in the garden and started to beat her with a section of hosepipe. When his two sons arrived home, he cut the hose in two. The other son went and found a stick so that all three could beat her. After two hours, she lost consciousness. Ice was put on the soles of her feet in an attempt to revive her and a pain-killing injection was given; both without success. Her uncle took her to hospital where she was pronounced dead. The subsequent post mortem revealed the cause of death to be a brain haemorrhage. An interesting additional piece of information, given the nature of her injuries, was the confirmation that she had not been sexually active.

The men's defence had been that it was not their intention to kill her, but simply to discipline her. This defence was accepted by the court. The original sentences were halved following representations by the rest of the family.

Having read this report, I was angrier than I had ever been. What sort of society was this, where the laws of the land accepted that a two-hour beating was an understandable albeit mildly punishable course of action, given the circumstances? This did not concern some ignorant men in a rural backwater. This had happened in the country's capital city; a vibrant boom-town with pretensions to international standards. Even as I write, it is reported that Afghan MPs have halted a debate on a new law concerning women's rights. After only 15 minutes all discussion was stopped. They failed to approve the law because parts of it violated Islamic principles. Among its provisions was a ban on child marriage and outlawing the practice of trading women to settle disputes.

In the company of both men and women, I started to say things like,

"Women are a lot more than their bodies, you know." Or,

"Our bodies are from Allah too." Or,

"There are parts of the world, like Tibet, where nudity is accepted naturally, and not as an indicator of improper sexual display." Or,

"There are parts of China, where the imams are female." Or,

"I just think that people should be able to live without fear." Or,

"There are communities in the north of India where it is the women who are allowed to take more than one husband." Or,

"If any given belief or message aspires to the status of self-evident truth, why does it need fear in order to instil or maintain it?"

The women listened, fascinated, their eyes lighting up at the dawning realisation of other ways of thinking, yet wondering at my audacity. Most of the men laughed at me. Just sometimes, there were one or two who nodded quietly but remained silent.

There *have* to be some absolutes which transcend religious dogma or cultural preference. Anything which seeks to suppress female energy, or to deny the equality of the genders has *got* to be wrong. The Five Pillars of Islam are wonderful guidelines for the conduct of human life. Are they not enough? Religious tolerance has become, in itself, too much of a sacred cow. I began to wonder...how would it be if all the cardinals or all the rabbis or all the archbishops or all the imams or any of the leaders of the world's great religions met together to review their teachings? How would it be if it were decided that recent scholarship of their holy texts had provided authority for them henceforth to require that women be confined to the home? Would the rest of us throw up our hands and say,

"We must respect this. This is their sincerely held belief."

What of the women themselves? Once a society has decided the criteria for a good woman, many women will want to meet those standards regardless of the effect they have on their lives or on their attitudes to their own bodies. Was it such a climate that had produced the apathy I had witnessed when Faisal, the disabled boy, was stoned? Must it be so; that men and women live their lives, afraid of each other? Enough was enough. I could not 'buy into' such a culture. How was I going to continue living in this world when I felt at such odds with the life around me?

It was then that news arrived from home which was to change everything. My son, a Royal Marine, was to be deployed to Afghanistan on a seven months tour of duty. I could not bear to be away from the United Kingdom while he was away. What if he were brought home injured or close to death? I had to be in a position where I could be with him quickly. And then there was Bassam. He has two sons. He has two small houses under his own. One is mine, the other is rented out. If I left, he would have two homes ready for both his sons when they were older.

I made the decision to leave. I went upstairs to tell Bassam and Fatma. Choking back the tears, I could barely get the words out. Fatma and I cried. Bassam left the room.

Chapter 18
Leaving

Word of my impending departure soon spread. Those I counted my friends were genuinely sad and worried, on my behalf, about my son. Others were quick to ask what I was going to do with the contents of my house.

"Well," I said, "I will just take my clothes and books with me. The rest I will sell because it will be expensive to air-freight my belongings."

"Why sell? You know that we are poor." [This from a woman whose husband had just spent over a thousand dinars on expensive ceramic tiles for the house they were preparing for their son.]

" Who is having your calor gas cylinder? Who is having your fan? Who is having your television?" Fatma came down.

"How much will you want for your Arabic seating, cooker and fridge-freezer?" she said. I gave her prices which were well below the going rate. Within two days, she had paid me the money to reserve them. In the end, I gave her a lot more because of her honesty and because she understood that I only wanted to raise the money that I needed and that I had no intention of trying to make a profit from my neighbours.

Amani, the starving neighbour whom I had tried to help with food and small alms, started to visit more frequently. She never went away empty-handed; sometimes a rug, another time a fan. I was invited to lunch at the home of her heavily pregnant neighbour. Amani was also invited. Throughout the meal, the two women told me how they needed twenty dinars for this or for that. I said,

"I cannot give money to every woman in the village." After that, their demands dropped to ten dinars. Still, at the end of the meal, I left without being persuaded to part with any money.

The very day before my departure, Amani came to visit me with her five-year old boy. By that time, I hardly had a stick of furniture left in the house. I was busy ironing on a white plastic table in my bedroom. She and her son sat on the bed. I brought them fruit juice. Chofa arrived from upstairs, partly for moral support and partly, I suspected, to ensure that Amani did not leave my house with anything destined for upstairs.

The ironing finished, I went through to the kitchen to prepare a salad for lunch. Chofa, Amani and her son followed me. None of them wanted to stay and eat with me. As I prepared the food, I filled a bag with unwanted items for Amani; rice, tea, flour and raisins. When my lunch was ready, Chofa took her leave. I sat down to eat and once again offered to share my food with Amani. No. She didn't want food. It was clear that she wasn't going to leave until I gave her some money. With my imminent departure, this was her last chance to extract money from me. She was clearly prepared to sit and wait and watch me eat my meal, until I gave her something. Finally, I left my seat at the table and collected my purse, hoping that I still had some small value notes. No. The smallest denomination I had was a ten dinar note. I took that out and offered it to her. She snatched it from my hand and left.

At various times during my nine years in Jordan, people in the UK would say to me,

"You won't change anything. You are wasting your time." I tried again to explain my attitude to my life in the village.

"I don't see myself as a one-woman-band," I would reply."I just hope that my presence in the village has sown some seeds in people's minds about how the lives of the women can be different. I just want to show the men that it is possible for a woman to be both more independent, and yet a good woman.

These were my hopes but, in my heart, I doubted that I had made any difference at all. People were not interested in learning anything from me. I offered to help with English lessons at the Girls' school. That offer was never taken up but could I provide exercise books and pencils? I did. I could have taught some of the women to drive, but that was a step too far. Instead, could I take them to lady doctors in Ma'an, Aqaba and Al Hissa? I did. Could I take their children to hospital? I did. Could I use my car to bring wheat and hay for their animals? I did.

I had earned titles of respect. *Um Peter*, mother of Peter and, more importantly, *Haja,* a term of respect usually reserved for women who have made the pilgrimage to Mecca. Despite such evidence to the contrary, had my nine years in the country simply been an eccentric excursion? It certainly felt like it.

A month after I left Jordan, I was Skyping some Ukrainian friends who live in Wadi Musa. They run a photographic studio for women. Two weeks before my departure, they had insisted that I went to the studio for a photo shoot. I submitted and was, indeed, pleased with the resulting images. As we talked, they lifted a photo frame from their window display and put it in front of the computer camera so that I could see it. It was one of the photographs they had taken of me. They said that several men had seen it, entered the studio and said,

"What is a picture of Joanna doing in your window?" One day, a man came in, pointed at the photograph, and said,

"I know her. That woman is the Angel of Petra."

956
WAR

Printed in Poland
by Amazon Fulfillment
Poland Sp. z o.o., Wrocław